MIA FARROW

Mia FARROW

FLOWER CHILD,
MADONNA,
MUSE

SAM RUBIN
RICHARD TAYLOR

2M Communications, Ltd.

ST. MARTIN'S PRESS
NEW YORK

Photo Research by Amanda Rubin
Design by Glen M. Edelstein

Library of Congress Cataloging-in-Publication Data
Rubin, Sam.
      Mia Farrow: flower child, madonna, muse / Sam Rubin and
      Richard Taylor.
      p.   cm.
      ISBN 0-312-02950-0
      1. Farrow, Mia, 1945-   . 2. Motion picture actors and
actresses—
      United States—Biography. I. Taylor, Richard, 1956-
      II. Title.
      PN2287.F35R8   1989
      791.43'028'0924—dc19
      [B]   89-30163

First Edition
10 9 8 7 6 5 4 3 2 1

For Julie, with all my love. Sammy

To Mom and Dad. Thanks for all your love and support. Richard

CONTENTS

ACKNOWLEDGMENTS

The authors would like to sincerely thank the following for their great assistance in the preparation of this work. We couldn't have done it without you, all of you.

Sharlene Adams; Betty Anderson; Elizabeth Anderson; Elmer Anderson; Mullane Anderson; Gordon Basichis; Kimberly Beck; Keith Black; Liz Blackman; Tony Brenna; Karen Bondi; Bill Dooley; Alix Doumakes; Debbie Doumakes; George Friedman; Marcia Friedman; Judith Guest; Cheryl Graves; David Graves; Andy Green; Norman Green; Stephen Green; Rachel Green; Alan Greenspan; Jack Haley, Jr.; John Hogg; Edward Horowitz; Charlie Horton; Jeff Hoyt; Allan Huntley; Jennifer Kawar; Julielle; Daniel Kessler; Mary Kirby; Chuck Krall; Audrey Lavin; Robb Madrid; Linda Mazur; Stephen H. Mazur; Leslie McCandless; Lauralee Mencum; David McGough; David Parry; Brian Panarese; Marianne Robin-Tani; David Ritchie; Anne Rubin; Buddy Rubin; Ted Rubin; Bill Schawbel; Scott Schneid; Jack Sher; Jill Shively; David D. Shumaker; Esther Sorkin; Ira Sorkin; Mark Steen; Michael M. Stoddard; Daisy Sylbert; Irving Taylor; Ken H. Tsuboi; Ethlie Ann Vare; Michael Waco; Karen Walton; and Sherry Weinman.

Acknowledgments

The exceptional contributions of the following are noted with great appreciation. Thanks to those below for your special efforts.

Francis Bustowne; Deborah Chenoweth; Audrey Friedman; Terri Hartman; Vanda Krefft; Stella Jane Mittelbach; Melissa Prophet; Sharmagne Leland-St. John; and Leona Taylor.

A special thanks to Maureen O'Sullivan for her delightful participation and help. And to literary agent Madeleine Morel, many thanks for her strength, cooperation, and good nature.

—Toni Lopopolo
Executive Editor

MIA FARROW

INTRODUCTION

$\mathcal{M}$IA Farrow has crowded several incredible lifetimes into one. Now forty-one, Mia has had three great and celebrated love affairs with three unique, world-famous men: Frank Sinatra, André Previn, and Woody Allen. Each relationship was vastly different, but every one left an indelible mark on Mia's development. And yet, even with these relationships, Mia has another side of her life that is more important: being a mother to her nine children.

Additionally, Farrow's enormously successful acting career has run the gamut from early achievement on television's *Peyton Place* to unforgettable performances in films as diverse as *Rosemary's Baby*, *Death on the Nile*, *Broadway Danny Rose*, and *The Purple Rose of Cairo*. While Farrow's life has made headlines for over two decades, few are aware of the private side of this highly unusual woman and the behind-the-scenes story of her life. Over the course of her career Farrow has made significant transformations. From her marriage to the significantly older Frank Sinatra to her work/love relationship with Woody Allen, and her career from Hollywood starlet to English country housewife to a New York working mother of nine, Mia has done it all. This is her story.

In this work we have elected to examine Mia's life and career first and then to present separately a comprehensive discussion of her films. It is our hope that this approach will allow you to fully understand both Mia Farrow the person and Mia Farrow the actress.

CHAPTER 1

ORIGINS OF AN ACTRESS

THE birth of the third child of actress Maureen O'Sullivan and film director John Farrow was uncomplicated. It may have been the only simple event of Mia Farrow's life. Propelled by her family legacy, Mia has fulfilled her incredible destiny to become one of the most controversial—onscreen and off—of all performers.

Maria de Lourdes Villers Farrow was born on February 9, 1945, in the southern California coastline city of Santa Monica. The birth merited notices in the nearby Los Angeles and Hollywood papers, for both John Farrow and Maureen O'Sullivan were well-known show-business veterans. Noted film director George Cukor and popular gossip columnist Louella Parsons, longtime friends of the family, were Mia's godparents. In hindsight, the choice of Cukor and Parsons was particularly symbolic, as Mia's life would dominate both the film screen and the gossip columns.

There's no doubt that Mia's radiance and talent can be traced directly to her parents. Irish-born Maureen Paula O'Sullivan's Hollywood career spanned more than forty years and included appearances in more than seventy films, including the classics *Anna Karenina, The Thin Man, Pride and Prejudice, The Big Clock,* and *A Yank at Oxford.* In spite of this impressive list of well-known films, O'Sullivan is best remembered as the original Jane in the classic *Tarzan* series, which ran from 1932 to the early 1940s. At the time, she was paid what was considered a king's ransom for her work in *Tarzan*—$300 per week.

O'Sullivan never achieved the true and lasting stardom that contemporary leading ladies like Katharine Hepburn and Ingrid Bergman enjoyed. O'Sullivan's starring roles were limited to B movies; in "serious" films, she was cast in secondary roles.

"I was never a success for three reasons," O'Sullivan recounted to entertainment writer David Galligan in 1981. "First of all I was insecure. I didn't have the fashionable looks of that time, say like Constance Bennett or Joan Crawford. Secondly, I felt inferior. Thirdly, I was always tied up shooting a *Tarzan* film. I missed many good roles because of that."

The "good roles" Maureen lost because of her *Tarzan* obligations included such classics as *Our Town* and *Wuthering Heights.* Her Hollywood career was undeniably a study in frustration—a direct contrast to her pleasant childhood, which could have been invented by Hollywood storytellers.

The daughter of a major in the British army, Maureen grew up in the beautiful village of Roscommon, Ireland. Director Frank Borzage, who was shooting a film on location in Ireland, spotted the eighteen-year-old O'Sullivan in the audience at the 1929 Dublin International Horse Show. Enchanted by her youth and charm, he cast her in his movie *Song O' My Heart*, starring the famous Irish tenor John McCormack.

Casting agents were mesmerized by O'Sullivan's debut, and she was quickly signed to a film contract with 20th Century-Fox. With her mother in tow, Maureen moved to Hollywood to become a star.

And star she did, in six films for Fox. But in addition to the lights and the cameras, Maureen was suddenly introduced to the fickle, often underhanded world of show-business deals. Maureen was being groomed to replace actress Janet Gaynor, who left because of a financial dispute with the studio. But Gaynor returned, and after completing the six films for Fox, Maureen was shocked to discover that the studio refused to renew her contract.

"They suddenly turned around and said they didn't want me anymore," Maureen revealed. "They said to me, 'You're not worth a dime.' There were no good-byes."

Maureen soon found a new niche—in the jungle, swinging on vines through the MGM studio backlot with Johnny Weissmuller in *Tarzan the Ape Man*. Maureen enjoyed working with her human costars—especially Weissmuller, with whom she became close friends—but she had unfriendly relationships with the animals: "Cheetah, that bastard, bit me whenever he could. The apes were all homosexuals, eager to wrap their paws around Johnny's thighs. They were all jealous of me and I loathed them."

While working on the *Tarzan* series, however, Maureen met John Farrow, a brilliant and handsome young Australian writer, who had been hired to grind out one of the many *Tarzan* sequels that the series demanded. Maureen and John married just a short time after they first met in 1936.

Maureen O'Sullivan endowed Mia with beauty and acting ability; John Farrow gave her more challenging gifts, contributing to her complex and often contradictory nature. Friends and colleagues agree that John Farrow was a man of brilliant intellect and eclectic interests. He was a distinguished and award-winning writer, director, and producer.

Farrow directed many films including *Five Came Back, A Bill of Divorcement, China, The Naked and the Dead, The Night Has a Thousand Eyes, A Bullet Is Waiting, John Paul Jones*, and *The Big Clock*, which starred O'Sullivan along with Ray Milland and Charles Laughton. The director was known not only for his work in film but for his controversial lifestyle; his reputation as a dashing ladies' man was no secret in Hollywood.

A fellow director said of his friend and mentor John Farrow, "He was a master of style and communication. There wasn't anything about the movies that he didn't know, and nothing on a set that he couldn't do. And movies were only one of his interests."

John was a man of many passions, including women. Despite his rigid Catholic views, his behavior would not qualify him for the priesthood.

Born in Sydney, Australia, in 1904, John Farrow was educated for a naval career. After several years in the Merchant Marines and an enlistment in the U.S. Marine Corps in Latin America, Farrow went to Tahiti to pursue his greatest love, writing. His first book, *Laughter Ends*, was published in 1934. Farrow also compiled an English-French-Tahitian dictionary.

Farrow left Tahiti and ventured to Hollywood, where he began his career as a screenwriter and met with immediate success, both personally and professionally. Among his first writing assignments was *Tarzan*, which led to the fateful meeting with the beautiful Maureen O'Sullivan. Farrow made the transition from professional writer to director when Warner Brothers signed him to direct his screenplay *My Bill*.

The movies were not enough to contain Farrow's wide range of interests, especially his fascination with the Roman Catholic Church. Having converted to Catholicism, he wrote extensively about religious subjects and the history of the Church. Farrow also wrote biographies of St. Ignatius Loyola and Sir Thomas More, and *Damien, the Leper*, which was translated into twelve languages.

For his works on figures in the Catholic Church, Farrow received many papal honors and was made a Knight of the Holy Sepulcher by Pope Pius XI. His works show Farrow to be an inquisitive scholar, and his interest in education extended to his involvement on the advisory board of Mount St. Mary's College and as a regent of Loyola University of Los Angeles.

In 1939, after Maureen and John's first son, Michael, was born, John left his young family to serve with the Royal Canadian Navy during World War II.

Farrow was an excellent leader and quickly rose in rank, receiving many decorations for his military service, including Commander of the British Empire. In 1941, Farrow was assigned to an antisubmarine vessel. While on board, he suffered a near-fatal attack of typhus.

A virtual invalid, Farrow was sent back to Beverly Hills. Under Maureen's devoted nursing, Farrow's health improved. In 1941 Paramount Pictures offered Farrow the opportunity to direct the film *Wake Island*. His physical and professional health returned while he worked on the movie. The following year Farrow won an Academy Award nomination for his directorial effort on the film.

After Mia's birth, Farrow kept up his hectic work schedule. During Mia's earliest years her father devoted himself completely to his professional life, gaining great respect in the film industry.

Farrow won an Academy Award in 1956 for best screenplay for cowriting *Around the World in Eighty Days*, the fanciful adventure-comedy starring David Niven, Shirley MacLaine, and Cantinflas, which also included forty-four cameo appearances by such stars as in Charles Boyer, John Gielgud, Trevor Howard, Buster Keaton, Marlene Dietrich, George Raft, and many others.

Mia loved and greatly respected her father. But she has said very little about him, as if withholding judgment in an attempt to fully understand his contradictory nature. She did say that her father "was a marvelous man, a paradox. He was remarkably knowledgeable. And tough, very tough. But he was gentle. He was many people at once, good and bad. He wanted to be the pope, a poet, and Casanova."

John Farrow also wanted a family, and he and Maureen had seven children together. Michael and Patrick were born before Mia; John, Prudence, Stephanie, and Tisa all followed her.

Their mother became a Beverly Hills housewife. Far from the glamour of her previous career, Maureen's life was now filled with the demands of her many children and the domestic chores a spacious home requires. Maureen excelled in this new domestic role and soon became involved in other activities far from the limelight of the film industry, serving as president of the St. John's Hospital Guild in Santa Monica and working for the social service auxiliary of her church, the Church of the Good Shepherd, in Beverly Hills.

In the fast-lane lifestyle of Hollywood the Farrow family was an anomaly. Said one old friend, "They stayed married. They kept having babies. They went to church. John worked on important films, and also on serious works on the papacy. They appeared to be so straitlaced—it was all very odd in film circles."

A Beverly Hills neighbor recalled, "The first time I saw Mia was at Catholic church, the Church of the Good Shepherd, every Sunday. The Farrows were a mighty army and they would all march to church every Sunday without fail. They were very religious, very devout Catholics."

After nearly a decade of going to church on Sunday and staying at home with the children, Maureen decided to come out of her self-imposed retirement to take advantage of a rare opportunity. She was offered a starring role in *The Big Clock*, which costarred Ray Milland and was directed by John Farrow. Maureen enjoyed working again and decided she would slowly resume her career, provided that she had enough time for her family's needs. Maureen was engaged in the delicate balancing act of career woman and mother, some thirty years before it became a common American practice.

Maureen next worked on the film *Mission over Korea* and was set to star in yet another movie when nine-year-old Mia contracted polio. When the delicate Mia became ill, her parents were naturally greatly alarmed. Mia had always been a thin and wispy child who relied on her imagination to see her through lonely periods. Before Mia could even speak she had developed a private world filled with characters of her own creation. Most notable of these characters was a girl named Mildred. Mia used Mildred as a stand-in imaginary friend who took the blame when things went wrong.

Though Mildred was a source of amusement for the family, Mia's parents were concerned that their daughter not live with her fantasy friends for too long. When Mia was six years old, the family was aboard a ship taking a vacation cruise. Her mother told her, "I tell you what we're going to do. We're going to drown Mildred." And they did. Mia never saw her again.

Fortunately, after a short stay at the hospital, Mia was able to overcome the illness. Doctors credited the child's strong will and John and Maureen's bedside support for Mia's quick recovery. Mia carries only one side effect with her today: a minor weakness in her left shoulder.

While Mia was physically able to beat polio, the disease took its emotional toll. All of the girl's possessions, including her most beloved toys and dolls, were gathered and burned to prevent the spread of the disease. "Even my magic box, full of things that were magical to me, was burned," recalled Mia.

Realizing that a serious illness, coupled with the destruction of her cherished toys, was an emotional upheaval for the delicate child, Mia's parents sent her to a psychotherapist. "I was an insomniac by the time I was eight,"

Mia recalls. "The bad times all came before I was twelve. That was the only period of sustained analysis. It was a jiffy course, in which someone tried to stick me together. . . . It's an incredibly fragile thread that we hang on to."

While Mia battled with health and emotional difficulties, she was never at a loss for creature comforts. Her early years were spent in a luxurious house on Beverly Drive in Beverly Hills. In addition to her mother, Mia also had three governesses who looked after her and her siblings. She attended an expensive Beverly Hills parochial school, Blessed Sacrament.

In her early teens, still recovering from the emotional shock of her polio battle, Mia decided that she wanted to become a nun. She said, "In my world—and it was a shaky world at best—I figured it was about the best thing that I could do.

"The time had come when I realized the shortness, the tininess of life, and I said to myself, 'Where can you, a ninety-eight-pound creature, fit in? If you're going to be on earth six weeks or six months or sixty years, you try to find something bigger than yourself. I decided that a nun would be a groovy thing to be."

While her intense quiet side desired the cloistered life, Mia's rambunctious, fun-loving side exhibited itself throughout her adolescent years. She developed a particularly crafty trick of using an old tooth to help her get out of class—and perhaps give her her first acting experience. Whenever Mia wanted a health pass to avoid school she would pull the old tooth out of her pocket, place it in her mouth, and wiggle it around, complaining to teachers of having a toothache. The tooth trick helped her skip class many times throughout the years.

In 1958, at age thirteen, Mia was uprooted by her father when he moved the entire Farrow family to Madrid, Spain, where he was to direct *John Paul Jones*. Mia and her brothers and sisters were sent to an American school in the city. Mia didn't last there for long. She recalls: "One day I shook up a seltzer bottle, aimed it at the ceiling and let go. I was thrown out of school."

Mia was then enrolled at the Santa Maria del Camino School in Madrid. "I didn't learn much—some Spanish, painting and drawing," Mia says, "and I had my ears pierced."

After a year in Spain, Farrow again moved his family, this time to England. Mia enrolled in an English convent school in Surrey, where her mischievous behavior earned her a reputation for being anything but devout. "I won the gym medal for leapfrog over three girls, and if I got suspended once, I got suspended twenty times," Mia said.

Mia had a series of run-ins with the nuns who were there to teach her. Once Mia brought an alarm clock, hidden in her school bag, to study hall. She placed the clock in a dark space and waited for it to go off. Mia's prank lasted a loud and long twenty minutes before the frightened nuns could find the clock and turn it off.

In addition to pranks, Mia further endeared herself to the nuns by conducting secret tours of their living quarters. Mia would persuade fellow schoolgirls to give her spare change and doughnuts while she would help them sneak around the cloistered areas where the nuns resided.

After one tour, Mia heard the sounds of some nuns approaching, and while she and her tour guests were trying to hide behind a curtain, the Mother Superior found them and punished Mia. "I was face-to-face with the Mother

Superior," Mia recalls. "They put me in solitary confinement."

Mia's initial desire to be a nun met with disapproval from the sisters of Surrey. One nun told her that she was far too wicked to ever join their ranks.

Her future as a nun may have been suspect, but during that period Mia gained experience in what was to become her true vocation: acting. At the convent school, she played the lead in the play *Amahl and the Night Visitors*. She also sang in the choir and acted in Christmas pageants. Mia recalled, "The school was old and freezing cold. But I made some wonderful friends."

Mia's happy, if mischievous, adolescence was shattered by the sudden and tragic death of her older brother Michael. On October 28, 1958, Michael was killed in a fiery and spectacular midair collision over Pacoima, California, some thirty-five miles from the family home. Michael had been taking flying lessons at college, and on this particular day the preset flight plan had been changed. Through a series of tragic miscommunications, Michael's plane was set on a collision course with another small plane. Two other men died in the crash.

Mia was hit particularly hard by her brother's untimely death. Michael's passing was the first death Mia ever encountered, and she was emotionally unequipped to deal with it. Michael and Mia had shared a very special relationship. She felt closer to this brother at times than to any other member of her family. Mia looked up to him as a role model and as surrogate father. Returning his sister's affection, Michael had affectionately dubbed her "Mouse." Just one week prior to the plane crash, Michael wrote to Mia, "Dear Mouse, I hope you are growing."

While the family gathered in Beverly Hills, Mia, devastated by the loss, refused to attend the funeral, choosing instead to grieve alone at the convent school in England. While Mia remained in England, two hundred mourners joined the Farrow family for the Requiem Mass at the Church of the Good Shepherd in Beverly Hills. John Farrow had been a member of the Marine Corps reserve, and a Marine Corps honor guard performed at the graveside.

Mia says of her brother's death, "It quite simply destroyed the family. He had been the closest person to me, my confidante, my idol. I worshipped him." The death had an effect on each member of Mia's family. The children, Mia said, "just sort of fell into our own plots of soil and grew."

Mia remained in England for two more years, dashing in and out of trouble at school, and testing the waters of acting in various plays and classes. Finally Maureen wrote Mia an impassioned letter begging her to return to Beverly Hills for her final year of high school.

Mia complied with her mother's request and enrolled at Marymount, a Catholic preparatory school for girls in West Los Angeles. At Marymount Mia's entire life changed, for she finally decided what she didn't want to become, and what she did.

At the age of sixteen, after serious consideration, Mia realized that she didn't want to become a nun after all. The California nuns were enough to convince Mia at last that she wasn't cut out for a life of the cloth: "The nuns in California turned me off. The nuns seemed to be more interested in raising money for the school than in answering my questions on religion." The glamour of the sisterhood was not what Mia had imagined: "I thought I would-be able to levitate and stuff and have visions. I used to go to church every morning—it was a very seductive religion," Mia recalled.

In spite of her boisterousness at convent schools, Mia was a shy teenager. Like most teenage girls, Mia was interested in boys but wasn't quite sure how to attract them. At a teenage dance at the Beverly Hills Hotel, Mia and another girl were wallflowers. They sat on the sidelines and watched all their other friends dance. Finally a boy came toward them. Mia's spirits were crushed as the boy turned to Mia's friend and asked for a dance.

Alone, Mia set about comparing herself to the other girls. She recalls, "I had no socks and no chest. The next day I went out and bought hose and falsies."

The new purchases didn't help much. Mia still didn't get involved with boys. Ever the pragmatist, she sought a place where she could get attention: the stage.

At Marymount Mia found the first tangible results of her acting work, and they whetted her appetite for more. She entered a National Forensic League competition involving seventy schools and walked away with a gold medal for her readings from *I Am a Camera* and *Our Town*. The acting bug had bitten Mia with a vengeance.

"I discovered that only in drama class could I manipulate people, amuse them, even make them notice me through this marvelous game of pretending, where I don't have to be me," she remembers. Onstage she could be a nun, an astronaut, or an underwater diver. The stage placed no limits on Mia's boundless imagination. She was ready to try and take Hollywood by storm.

But her father would have none of it. John Farrow had seen firsthand the abusive treatment the vast majority of

actresses receive, and he had no desire to let his daughter
attempt a career that could be so cruel. Even if she were
to achieve a level of success, John Farrow feared Mia
would face the same sense of disappointment that her
mother had felt at not being able to go all the way to
the top of her profession. Mia remembers her father's
objection. "He said he never saw a happy actress and sent
me off again to England to keep me away from the Hollywood environment."

Maureen did not want to see her daughter leave again
but was unable to put up much of a fight against John.
Seventeen-year-old Mia was again off to England to attend
the Cygnet House, a posh finishing school in London.
Away from the acting opportunities that she had grown
to love, Mia was bored to tears.

"The finishing school nearly finished me," Mia recalls.
Mia had little interest in learning how to select the proper
wine or how to coordinate a dining table set; her true
interests lay in the theater. While her instructors were telling their charges how to dress, Mia was dreaming of lavish
costumes that she could wear onstage.

Mia spent only a few months at the finishing school.
Maureen was acting again and was now in New York,
away from John's dictatorial influence, and starring for
her first time on Broadway in the comedy *Never Too
Late*.

Mia went to visit her mother during a break at school
and begged her to allow her to live in New York full time
to pursue acting. Maureen finally granted her daughter's
wish.

Mia's youth was filled with the joy of youthful
fantasy—and the sharp pain of real-world reality. But

when Mia left London to move to New York at the tender age of seventeen, no one could predict that she was ready to take the real world by storm. Not only would Mia Farrow make a name for herself, she would soon become a household name.

CHAPTER 2
THE RISE OF A STAR

*M*IA, fiercely independent from the start, was determined to become a success in her own right. She told an interviewer, "I've learned to rely on nobody but me, because that's all there is really. You were born alone, you live alone, you die alone."

Mia's remarks may have been prophetic. Her father died just as Mia's career started to take off. Falling victim to a massive heart attack, John Farrow died in the family's Beverly Hills home. Maureen was in New York performing in *Never Too Late* when word came of her husband's death. She immediately left New York for California to arrange for a funeral with a High Mass for her husband. Mia could not bring herself to leave New York to attend the funeral.

She told her mother that she could best say good-bye to her father in her heart.

A few years later, Mia did go to the cemetery where both her father and her brother Michael were buried. She recalled the visit: "When I got close to the burial plot they suddenly turned on the lawn sprinklers. I started to run, trying to avoid getting wet and trying to find my father and my brother's graves. When I located them I stood there for about five seconds, the sprinklers drenching me, and then ran away.

"The visit to the graves wasn't important to me. What is important is what both my brother and father meant to me. The lessons that I have learned from them both will always be with me, and in that way they will always be with me."

Maureen O'Sullivan said of her husband's death, "John died shortly after our twenty-seventh wedding anniversary. It was a terrible time for all of us. We'd been a close family and done so many things together. Suddenly I was overwhelmed by decisions I had to make about my own life and the children and schools and money and where to live. I'm a very orderly person, and at first I wanted to settle everything at once. I wanted to tie up the loose ends and make everything orderly."

Mia wanted to take care of herself. Remaining in New York, she went from being a complete unknown to becoming one of the top young actresses of her time in a matter of months. The transition from schoolgirl to cover girl occurred just before her nineteenth birthday. "At age eighteen, I didn't realize what I was getting into," Mia said. "My father had died, I had lots of brothers and sisters, and I wanted to help my mother and go out and find a job, at least for a couple of years. And then I never went back to school. I missed a big opportunity, not getting more of a formal education, but I don't think about that anymore."

Mia credits her July 1963 casting as Cecily in an off-Broadway production of *The Importance of Being Earnest* as her big break. Mia told *Daily Variety*'s Dave Kaufman that she got the part all by herself. "I stood in line," Mia said. "And I was picked out of fifty girls. I don't know why I was picked out. Perhaps it was timing, perhaps because it was the kind of part for which they said I was good. There were no strings, no pull. My parents being in show business meant nothing. The producers didn't know until after I was signed who my parents were."

Soon the entire New York theater community would know who Mia was. However, a bizarre roadblock stood in her way. While Mia's stage debut was dazzling, it took place during a newspaper strike in New York City, so the rave reviews were delayed until the strike was settled.

Despite the initial lack of printed praise, the word quickly circulated among New York's theatrical elite that this new actress was someone of serious merit. Actress Vivien Leigh was so taken with Mia's performance that she told dozens of her influential friends about the talented newcomer. Leigh's private raves soon were seconded by excellent public notices.

Studio talent scouts, hungry to sign up new performers to fill the ever-expanding needs of television and film casting, went to see Mia perform. Just a few weeks after her stage debut, Mia was signed by 20th Century-Fox for an exceptional five-picture deal and a starring role in the new television series *Peyton Place*.

Mia's work in the *Peyton Place* pilot caught the eye of

studio president Darryl F. Zanuck, and before shooting on the series started, he sent Mia to England as a last-minute replacement for Britt Eklund in the film *Guns of Batasi*. Mia loved working on the movie and relished her vamplike role. "I played a seductress," she told an interviewer at the time. "It's marvelous being a seductress."

She was well received in her film debut and, despite her young age, was regarded by the cast and crew as a true professional. There were no schoolgirl hysterics on the set. Mia had come to do good work, and that was what she did. Playing a seductress was excellent preparation, for in her next role Mia seduced all of America as she became the most popular young television actress of her time.

It didn't take long after the September 15, 1964, debut of *Peyton Place* on ABC for Mia Farrow to firmly establish herself in the hearts of millions of viewers. Her character, Allison MacKenzie, served as the sympathetic and dramatic focus of the highly controversial series. While critics called the show "obscene," "indecent," and "lurid," there was still plenty of praise for Mia.

The series was based on a novel by Grace Metalious, which had spawned a successful film version in 1957. In the film, actress Diane Varsi played Allison and became a popular star because of the role. However, Varsi didn't like the constant prying of the press and other shackles of stardom, and she left Hollywood prior to the beginning of the TV series.

When *Peyton Place* became a television series, it was a new and innovative concept in television drama. There had never been a continuing drama in prime time before. Nor had the subjects that were staples of life in Peyton Place—frigidity, infidelity, and children out of wedlock—been shown on a regular basis. *Peyton Place* was chock-full of scandal, and audiences absolutely loved it. The show quickly shot to third place in the national ratings, and the stars of the series, especially Mia Farrow, became instant national celebrities.

Mia was perfectly cast to play the long-suffering Allison. The character was a deeply troubled illegitimate teenager. Wispy, pale, freckle-faced Mia was ideal for the role. One of *Peyton Place*'s directors, Walter Doniger, told *Newsweek* that Mia was the right girl for the part, and for the times. Doniger said, "The girl reflects something in the culture. She wants to grow up; on the other hand she's afraid to. She's a girl in search of herself."

Allison MacKenzie's search for herself was watched by millions on a twice-a-week basis. *Peyton Place*'s success opened the door for several other nighttime dramas. *Dallas, Dynasty*, and *Knots Landing* would never have been possible without *Peyton Place*.

Mia herself realized exactly what the show was and wasn't. She told *Newsweek* at the time that the romantic drama of the show didn't bother her. "Sex is a problem of our age," Mia said. "Allison is naive. She wants to learn. She has a quest for knowledge about such things as sex, I guess. I put myself in that place. *Peyton Place* is good experience for me. Tragedy is a great thing to play. And it's number three in the ratings. There are few great moments for me in this. But those moments are worth it. An entire career is worth it for those moments. They are little moments of truth."

Mia's mother was not quite as enthusiastic about the series. When she first watched *Peyton Place* with some family and friends she was shocked: "We all thought that the show was dreadful. We all sat around and said, 'Who's going to tell her?' "

Maureen didn't have to speak up for Mia to realize the shortcomings of the series. Some fifteen years later, in a 1977 interview, Mia said, "*Peyton Place* was a terrible series. I thought it would last a couple of weeks. To my horror and astonishment it was a hit."

Mia did realize the constraints imposed by working on a series. She said in 1965, "When this is over, I will have finished with TV. My plans don't include TV, only pictures and the stage. I'm not knocking this series, but I'm a free soul. I like to pick and choose my own material. You forfeit that choice in a series. You can't pick and choose each script."

Mia made the best of it while on *Peyton Place*. Her friend Jack Haley, Jr., recalls visiting Mia on the set. "I was near Fox one day so I decided to go by the set to see Mia and my god-daughter Kimberly Beck, who was about ten years old at the time and played a child on the show.

"Mia and Kimberly were very close. Kimberly looked at Mia like a big sister, and Mia was always sweet and helpful to her. She was a real role model. But since both Mia and Kimberly were young, they would get into trouble together.

"I arrived on the set and I asked some of the crew where Kimberly was. I was told that she was over at the bedroom set. I went over to this big bedroom set and in this huge big bed were Kimberly and Mia. They were jumping around, just playing on the big bed, like kids at a grandmother's house. They just looked like little angels. When I think of how wonderful Mia was with Kimberly, you could tell even then what a great mother Mia Farrow would make."

Kimberly Beck, now thirty-two and an actress working in many popular television commercials and feature films, recalls working with Mia. "Mia had an unbelievable effect on my life. She was my role model. I idolized her, and I still do. I had a crush on her.

"She was very important in my life. I have the softest spot in my heart for her. I met her during my most impressionable years. Mia is so special to me. I wouldn't be the person I am today if it wasn't for her.

"Mia, who was the star of the show, the real up and comer, didn't have to take so much extra time to be so nice to me, but she did. She used to tell me I was magic, and then she would tell me stories about leprechauns and things when she was growing up.

"I was brought up in a very white-bread, middle-class upbringing. And here was Mia, and she was so ethereal and spiritual, and I had never experienced that before. Even at that time, I could see that Mia was a true artist. I know that sounds hard to believe with both Mia and I being so young at that time, but it's true. Mia had a very distinct philosophy.

"Even then, Mia knew that life isn't all about going to work and making enough money to put food on the table. Life is more than pragmatism.

"Mia would also share with me on the set stories about growing up. She said that when she was my age, she was a real troublemaker. She told me once about how she stuck a tack in her brother's foot. Even now I keep my feet covered when I sleep because I think someone could stick something in my foot. Mia made her story so vivid to me.

"Mia had a white four-door Jaguar, and she used to drive me around the set and sometimes take me off the lot for little field trips. One time we went to a wishing pond at a Chinese restaurant in Beverly Hills, and we made wishes with pennies. I asked her what her wish was and she said,

'I wished that no one would recognize me.' And then I said that I wished that everyone would recognize me. We both laughed a lot after I said that."

The success of *Peyton Place* sent scribes all over Hollywood in search of stories on Mia. Magazines from *Look* to *Teen* wanted to tell their readers all about America's newest bright young star. The profiles all came back with much the same story. Mia's life was simple and not particularly interesting: she lived alone in a small Beverly Hills apartment with her cat Malcolm, she rode her bike or took the Jaguar to the nearby 20th Century-Fox lot for a 6:30 A.M. studio call, and her favorite foods included ice cream and corn flakes.

Mia's life may have been prosaic, but her observations were wild and controversial. A profile on Mia produced so-so material, while actual quotes from the actress generated great copy.

Mia projected the youthful optimism of the early 1960s. Mia told *Look* magazine in a 1965 interview, "I'm like a kaleidoscope. I see a different person every time I look in a mirror." She told columnist Marilyn Beck, "I fall in love all the time. Falling in love is compulsive with me. I think everyone needs love, don't you?"

Mia also made this provocative statement about having both male and female friends: "I like both men and women, but I like men more. Maybe that's because men like me more. You can have so much more fun with men, don't you think? I know that I have. Whenever I fall in love, it's forever. Even if I end up hating that person, I continue to love him."

Kimberly Beck remembers that sometimes Mia regretted what she told the press. "On one of our little field trips during a shooting break, Mia and I drove to a newsstand to pick up some magazines. Mia was in almost every one of them.

"She was reading one particular piece while she was driving on the Sunset Strip, when she saw something that she didn't like. I remember her saying, 'Oh those idiots, look what they've written about me.' And she got so mad, Mia suddenly drove up the street's island."

Mia not only gave off wild and highly quotable remarks. Some of her off-camera behavior also reflected that same wildness.

One of Mia's closest friends during her rocket rise to stardom was the noted Spanish artist Salvador Dali, whom she would remain close to for years. Dali and Mia met in Manhattan before she was cast in *The Importance of Being Earnest*. Mia was on her way to a party and rode in an elevator with Dali. An immediate chemistry developed between the older artist and seventeen-year-old Mia. He asked her whether she liked elevators; she smiled and told him that she did. Mia and Salvador's friendship was formed as they rode that same elevator up and down its full run six times.

From that first meeting, Dali became a virtual father figure to Mia, and they saw each other in New York almost every day. They would regularly meet at the King Cole Bar of the St. Regis Hotel and enjoy afternoon tea together. Mia said of Dali, "I believe him. If he says so, it is true. Dali brought me out. He taught me the world is what you make of it. Who says it has to be four walls, three windows, and a rug on the floor? That's called convention—good for the masses and for the order of things—but I don't want it written on my tombstone."

Mia became so fond of Dali that when, two years after their meeting, as a nineteen-year-old star in Hollywood she purchased a horse for riding, she named the horse Salvador.

The New York adventures that Mia and Dali shared provided an informal education in worlds that she never explored while attending convent schools. During one particularly strange odyssey, Dali invited Mia to accompany him to a Greenwich Village party.

As they entered the party, they discovered, to Dali's amusement and Mia's shock, that the guests were mostly naked. Salvador had taken Mia to an orgy.

Mia later recalled the event. She said, "I wore my long white dress [and looked] like something that just arrived from heaven. We just stood there and watched. The guests were so deeply involved with themselves. I had a strange feeling that they were performing a ballet. I was so impressionable in those days, and I honestly still don't know exactly what they all were doing."

Back in Hollywood, Mia was about to get the romantic education of a lifetime. Some two years after witnessing the orgy with Dali, Mia's life had changed greatly. She was a major star, earning what was for the time an astounding salary of $50,000 a year.

Mia was so busy working on *Peyton Place* at the 20th Century-Fox studios that she didn't have much opportunity to enjoy the luxuries that her salary could easily afford her. Nor was she seen out often on the social circuit. She occasionally would date a rather unknown actor named John Leyton, but for the most part Mia kept to herself.

Says Kimberly Beck, "Mia was a big star and was treated well on the set, but she was getting tired of *Peyton Place*. There was a lot of the 'star stuff' Mia just didn't like. She never wanted to have makeup put on her. She wanted her real natural freckles to show through, but of course the director would tell her she had to have the makeup, and Mia went along.

"Unlike a lot of young actresses, Mia wasn't the least bit vain. She didn't like the chore of having to wash her hair every day, so sometimes she would just wash the bangs. It sounds like a little thing now, but if the hairdressers on the set knew about that, they would have thrown a fit.

"Mia also tired of the hours, which were very long. She would have shared with me stories about boys, but she hardly had time to meet any. For the most part Mia was pretty much alone socially. But all that changed when she met Frank."

Mia's period of apparent solitude ended abruptly. Her newest romance would make her even more famous and would prove to be the most widely reported romance west of Buckingham Palace. For while Mia was working at Fox, at a nearby sound stage a celebrity of far, far greater renown was also at work. His name was Frank Sinatra. After a whirlwind courtship that scandalized the entire country, he would later take Mia to be his bride.

There are many differing accounts of the first meeting between Mia and Frank Sinatra. As Frank's own daughter Nancy Sinatra remembers the meeting, Mia was walking over to the set of Sinatra's film *Von Ryan's Express*, which was just a few stages away from where *Peyton Place* was filming: "Father told me Mia looked absolutely radiant. She was dressed in a sheer white dress and looked like an angel."

Mia herself told *McCall's*, "When I had free time, I would hang around the *Von Ryan's Express* set. I remember that Edward Mulhare was there, and so was Frank Sinatra.

I would see Frank again and again, and it got to the point where I would say 'Hello, Mr. Sinatra.'

"One day I was playing around and one of Frank's friends came up to me and asked, 'Hey, kid, how old are you?' And I said, 'That's hardly a question to ask a lady.'

"Then he and Frank asked me to sit with them. And then Frank asked me to a screening of one of his pictures."

Mia was about to enter one of the most volatile periods of her life. In less time than it takes most girls her age to complete their college education, Mia had graduated from unknown to stage actress, movie star, and television sensation. But now she was entering an arena that no amount of experience or preparation could have possibly readied her for: love and marriage to Frank Sinatra.

CHAPTER 3
MRS.
FRANK SINATRA

$\mathcal{M}$IA'S relationship with Frank Sinatra was a gossip columnist's dream. Even the most outrageous Hollywood reporter would find it hard to imagine a pairing more likely to grab the interest of every fan. Mia was a rising star—and Frank Sinatra was the consummate superstar. For more than two decades he had absolutely dominated radio, concert halls, and films. There wasn't a bigger star in the American constellation.

"The Voice," "St. Francis," and "The Chairman of the Board"; all America knew Sinatra by his nicknames. Much more than just a big-band singer, Sinatra was a legend who had been entertaining the public with his professional work and personal exploits for years. Just short of his fiftieth birthday, Frank met the woman who would become his third bride—a woman young enough to be his daughter.

Mia made no secret of the fact that at this stage in her life, in spite of her television success, she wanted more. She told Hedda Hopper, "I want a big career, a big man, and a big life. You have to think big." Short of dating the pope, Mia couldn't have chosen a man bigger than Frank Sinatra.

The age difference was only one of a host of contrasts between the star-crossed pair. Frank was an old-fashioned man in his likes, preferring Italian food, boxing matches, and gambling, while Mia's pleasures included '60s trends such as health foods, mysticism, and ESP. Physically the two were starkly different. Wispy ninety-eight-pound Mia wore simple, chic minismocks; Frank favored expensive custom-made suits.

Mia purposely set out to meet Sinatra, and soon her personality and beauty genuinely captivated him. The feeling was mutual, although Mia claims that she couldn't understand her appeal to him. "I've always wondered what he saw in me," Mia said. "All I can remember is that suddenly I started being careful what I said to him."

Certainly she was saying the right things, because shortly after their first meeting on the set, Frank started to ask her out. On one of their early dates, the couple took Sinatra's private jet to his lavish Palm Springs home.

One close friend of the couple recalled, "Frank and Mia's romance took off like a rocket. And it was a funny thing, because Frank was nearly thirty years older, but he started courting Mia like he was in high school all over again.

"He was determined to win Mia over, and he did that by taking her everywhere. Frank took Mia to parties, to top restaurants, to movie screenings, to all the glittering

Hollywood events that any young star would give their eyeteeth to attend.

"It didn't take long for Frank and Mia to get together romantically. He started calling the set of *Peyton Place* virtually every day to check up on her, and she spent nearly every weekend with him in Palm Springs.

"Frank and Mia were falling very much in love, despite the obvious differences. She's much classier than Sinatra. You know, Frank's a terrific guy, but he isn't a class act. Mia is, and he knew it." Frank had found someone he wanted to hold on to, and he wasn't about to let go.

It was only six weeks after they first met that Mia and Frank's romance became fodder for Hollywood's top gossips. Mia herself broke the news to writer Sheilah Graham. Over lunch in late November 1964, Mia received a telephone call from Sinatra. She bounced back to the table to tell Graham that she had never been happier, because she had just received a call from someone that she was in love with.

It didn't take long for Graham to piece the rest of the details together, and in a column that appeared nationally, Graham wrote, "Frank Sinatra and Mia Farrow are the maddest, merriest romance of the year."

After Graham broke the news, Hollywood reporters and fans all over the country were hungry for a more detailed account of the new romance. But Frank and Mia, perhaps regretting that they had tipped their hand, would have none of it. After the Graham article, both spent months publicly denying that they were anything more than just good friends.

Dolly Sinatra, Frank's mother, was quoted as saying, "This Mia, she's a nice girl but that's all. My son is helping this girl become a star."

Mother doesn't always know best, however. With denials continuing to be issued from both camps, Frank and Mia were growing closer and closer.

At the time Mia lived in the luxury guest house of Saul and Helen Berner, in the Brentwood area of Los Angeles. Helen Berner recalled, "My husband and I have a very nice cottage next to our home, and for years some of the most important names in Hollywood have lived there. We are very respectful of their need for privacy, so I was happy to give Mia, who was so well known at the time, a quiet place to live.

"Mia shared the two-bedroom cottage with a personal secretary. It's a very nice place, with its own swimming pool.

"It was very clear when Frank Sinatra would come calling, and he would come a lot. He would pull up in a fancy sports car, and then there would be a second car with a few bodyguards in it.

"Mia knew that my husband and I didn't much care for the bodyguards, so she would just dash out the minute she saw Frank. Mia was very considerate that way. We really liked her a lot. We're very fussy about our property and make an effort to keep everything in order. If someone would throw paper on the driveway, Mia would pick it up. She's quite a lovely girl. Sinatra certainly must have thought so—he was here all the time picking her up, and off they would go on one of their many, many dates."

Kimberly Beck stayed friendly with Mia, even as her romance with Sinatra became more intense. Recalls Beck, "I first met Frank on Halloween. I went trick-or-treating at his house and he gave me a candy apple with a silver dollar. I thought that was the most incredible gift.

"I used to stay with Mia sometimes during the week-

ends, even when she was involved with Frank. Frank had
rented a house in Beverly Hills. Neither Frank nor Mia
lived there full time, but Frank allowed Mia to stay there
when she wanted to. The house had a great pool and we
used to go swimming.

"Mia used to have a deaf Persian cat named Malcolm.
Once he somehow got into some ink and walked all over
the rented house. We just laughed about it."

As Mia and Frank spent increasing amounts of time
together, they each seemed to change. Mia started behaving less outlandishly. She continued to speak to the press,
but not about her love life, and she also stopped making
curious otherwordly comments about her own career. Sinatra also changed; while his new girlfriend was very youthful, he seemed to mature. He started hanging out with a
new crowd of older performers and friends. Mia, thirty
years his junior, was the only person younger than he
whom Frank spent any time with.

One of the most curious aspects of their courtship was
their habit of dropping in to the popular disco the Daisy on
Rodeo Drive in Beverly Hills. The Daisy was one of the
hottest nightspots for the younger set, and Mia and Frank's
visits there often reminded others of a parent taking his child
to an amusement park. While Frank would sit with his glass
of scotch, he would watch Mia dance with her friends.

Jack Haley, Jr., the award-winning producer of many
television and film features including the popular MGM
That's Entertainment series, was one of Mia's dance partners. "It was a crazy circumstance," Haley recalls. "Mia
was more than willing and able to communicate with
Frank's friends, no matter how much older they were than
her. But Frank didn't really feel comfortable with any of
Mia's younger friends. So Frank would take her to the

Daisy, sit there like a stone, and watch Mia dance with other guys. You had the feeling, though, that Mia made sure that Frank knew exactly who she was dancing with, and that he had given his okay. No matter how much anyone liked Mia, no one wanted to upset Frank."

As their romance continued and the press peeled away the veneer of secrecy, many of Frank's friends teased him about the romance with Mia, especially considering that Mia was much younger than Frank's own children. Fellow "Rat Pack" member Dean Martin said, "I've got scotch older than Mia Farrow." Singer Eddie Fisher joked, "Frank didn't have to buy Mia a diamond ring; he gave her a teething ring." Mia herself let it be known that she had a nickname for Frank. She called him "Charlie," because when he would wrinkle his brow, Mia felt he looked like the popular comic strip character Charlie Brown.

In her authoritative biography of Frank Sinatra, *His Way*, author Kitty Kelley says that Frank was irritated by the comments of comic Jackie Mason. Mason had incorporated Mia and Frank's romance into his act and suggested that their nightly ritual involved "Frank soaking his dentures, while Mia brushes her braces . . . then she takes off her roller skates and puts them next to his cane . . . he peels off his toupee and she unbraids her hair."

Publicly Frank called Jackie Mason "a creep," but that was the least of Mason's problems stemming from the remarks. He received anonymous calls threatening his life if he didn't stop telling the Mia and Frank jokes. When he didn't alter his material at all, a gunman fired three shots through a patio door into Mason's Miami hotel room. Mason was unharmed, but a short while later another thug managed to get to him and punched the comic, damaging his nose and cheekbones.

Mason continued with his jokes and was unable to link Sinatra directly to the acts of violence. But Mason was sure there was a link. He summed up his feelings for Sinatra by telling Kelley, "He's a bum."

Despite being the butt of jokes all over America, Frank proudly introduced Mia to many of his friends, and she began to hang out with his crowd. She had already met many of the same people in her living room as a child. Maureen O'Sullivan said, "The people she now sees with Frank were guests in our home when she was a little girl."

The romance continued to bloom, and Frank invited Mia on her most spectacular social outing ever. In August 1965, Frank chartered a 168-foot yacht to cruise the New England coast and invited Mia and nine of his friends to join him for the trip.

The press had an absolute field day. Speculation was rampant that this was more than just a fancy boat ride: editors stood at the ready to piece together huge stories about Mia and Frank's wedding cruise. There was such intense interest in the couple's trip that *Time* magazine noted, "It was the most closely watched voyage since Cleopatra floated down the Nile to meet Mark Antony."

Others were not as excited about the prospect of a wedding. Maureen O'Sullivan was widely reported to have said, "If Mr. Sinatra is going to marry anyone, he ought to marry me." Sinatra's former wife, actress Ava Gardner, said, "I always knew Frank would wind up in bed with a little boy."

The cruise did not result in a wedding, but it did produce thousands of photographs of Frank and Mia together which were published in magazines and newspapers all over the country. Mia's personal life was far and away overshadowing her professional work. The *Peyton Place* producers could only sit back and watch the romance take off, not knowing whether their leading lady, whose real life was far more interesting than any romantic soap opera, was planning to return to the show.

The relationship between Mia and Frank had many rough spots. Prior to a big birthday bash for Frank, Mia decided to have her long hair cut. Next to Samson and Delilah's little adventure, it was, perhaps, the most widely reported haircut in history.

Noted stylist Vidal Sassoon performed the radical bob cut, which left Mia looking like a young tomboy. Her friend Salvador Dali commented to the press that in having her hair so severely cut, Mia "was committing mythical suicide."

Sinatra hated the hairstyle, so much that he quickly un-invited Mia to a large birthday party being thrown for him. Jack Haley, Jr., who produced the birthday bash, recalled, "The night that Mia cut all her hair off, Frank just up and decided that he wouldn't take her to the party. Different couples have different ways of getting to each other. The haircut and Frank's reaction were the simple and definite signs of stress in their relationship.

"After the birthday party for Frank, I went with some friends to the Daisy. I pulled off the bow tie I was wearing and was sitting in one of the big comfortable swivel chairs they had there.

"All of a sudden this body just hurls right into my lap. I thought it was an overly aggressive newsboy trying to give me a paper. I thought to myself, 'What the hell is going on here? Why is this young boy just sitting in my lap?'

"Of course after a moment I realized it was Mia. She had cut off all of her long, beautiful hair.

"I could tell that she was somewhat embarrassed by what she had done. But, and this is typical of Mia, once she had done it, she wasn't about to hide from anybody.

"In fact, she wanted to show it to the world."

Mia's new short hair was all the rage at the Daisy, and once photos of the new bob circulated in newspapers all across the country, thousands of women begged their hair stylist for "the Mia cut."

Jack Haley, Jr., believes that Mia "cut her hair as an act of defiance. She wanted to let him [Frank] know that she could make waves on her own, that he wasn't the only one calling the shots.

"It's difficult to imagine the shock Mia's cut caused. This famous, famous woman had long, beautiful hair practically down to her ankles. And now it was gone.

"But Mia kept her great wits about her. I saw her on a Sunday night, and she said to me, 'Now what am I going to do on *Peyton Place* tomorrow? The producers are going to kill me.' "

Certainly the *Peyton Place* producers were surprised. One executive said, "Mia's haircut caused quite a problem. Our viewers were used to seeing her one way, and now, suddenly, she is quite another way. It was almost like a sex change."

But the producers, thrilled with the seemingly unending press that Mia's life generated, were happy to have the actress still on board the show at all. Their happiness was short-lived, however. Mia's contract expired in the spring of 1966, and despite generous offers to get her to return to the show, Mia stated that she had no interest in staying with the series. She left the program, and though her character was vital to the continuing story, producers did not replace her with another actress, choosing instead to have the character of Allison mysteriously disappear.

Frank and Mia were able to patch up their romance and continued dating on an even heavier basis. They were practically inseparable, spending almost every weekend at his Palm Springs home.

Finally, after months of intense speculation in the press, Frank and Mia were married. Helen Berner recalls the start of the big day in July 1966: "All of a sudden there was a security guard posted on our driveway. We were used to big productions before Frank came to pick Mia up on a date, but there was never anything like this before.

"A few fans of Mia's would often hang around the house hoping to catch a peek at her, but on this particular day the guards just chased everyone away.

"One of the guards questioned my own son and some of his friends as they were trying to come into our house. It was clear that security was a top priority for Sinatra. He didn't want anything to happen to his bride-to-be.

"Frank came in a big fancy car this time and went in for Mia, who came out with quite a few pieces of luggage. The bodyguards loaded everything up, and Mia and Frank went off.

"Both my husband and I knew that Mia and Frank were off to Las Vegas to get married. Before she left, she told us that she wouldn't be needing the cottage anymore. It was clear what she meant. She and Sinatra had been getting closer all the time."

Flanked by bodyguards, Mia and Frank jetted to Las Vegas. In a four-minute ceremony at the glitzy Sands Hotel, the couple exchanged vows. The wedding was witnessed by dozens of still and motion picture cameramen, but no members of either the Farrow or Sinatra families were present. Frank sealed his vows by giving Mia a nine-carat diamond ring that was reported to be worth $84,000. The newlyweds had a quiet dinner and then began their lives as the era's most closely watched married couple in America.

They moved into a beautiful home in the Bel Air neighborhood of Los Angeles, and much as Maureen O'Sullivan had set about creating a home for John Farrow, Mia began to decorate the home for Sinatra. He was fond of bright yellow, orange, and white, and Mia incorporated these colors into her designs. Much of the furniture for the house was custom made, based on Mia's drawings. She preferred pieces in an English country style and ordered a lot of wooden furniture. Despite her unlimited budget she often had troubled communicating to furniture companies exactly what she wanted. She commented on a particular irony: "One manufacturer didn't understand what I wanted at first. Now he has a 'Mia Table' in his catalogue."

Their home life was very simple. Mia and Frank would listen to music—including their favorites, the Beatles—and watch films and television. Mia told the prying press that their home life was not much different from anyone else's. "We have a quiet life at home," she reported.

But not all was quiet. After the marriage Mia received incredible amounts of hate mail from fans of Sinatra's and others who did not approve of the May-December marriage. In one particularly frightening incident a lavishly decorated cake was delivered to the Sinatra home. Mia was suspicious about the gift because there was no return address. She ordered that the cake be taken from the home and tested in a lab. Mia's fears proved all too justified: the cake was chock-full of arsenic. Lab technicians told her that just a few bites would have been fatal.

The difficulty with sick and cruel fans affected Mia's behavior. Sinatra was tough and aggressive and always had hired muscle with him to back up his demeanor, but the wispy Mia sometimes was genuinely afraid for her safety and, as always, she was concerned about her privacy.

Mia traveled without Frank to London to make the movie *The Secret Ceremony* with Elizabeth Taylor. While there, Mia, Taylor, Richard Burton, and Robert Mitchum were all having dinner. At Mia's suggestion the foursome wrote a long postcard to send back to the States, but Mia, fearful of her privacy being compromised, refused to put the postcard in a mailbox. She told the other dinner guests, "I can't get up and mail this card. If someone sees me do it, they'll fish out the card and read it themselves."

Shortly after they were married, Sinatra's father died. Jack Haley, Jr., recalls, "Frank went to Hoboken ahead of us, and his daughter Nancy, who I was engaged to at the time, and Mia and I went together. I picked Mia up, and then I picked up Nancy and we all flew to New Jersey together.

"On the way to the airport, Mia had a Mason jar with a couple of pet turtles in it. She said, 'Jack, could you stop? I want to get some dirt for the turtles.'

"So I stopped the car and Mia got out and picked up some dirt to put in this jar. I believe she took the turtles with her all the way to the funeral. Mia was funny that way. She was very mature in some ways and very childlike in others. She was a walking contradiction."

After Mia and Frank returned to California from the funeral, Mia decided to continue working without long breaks between projects, and troubles with Sinatra really began. Author Kitty Kelley reports that when they were back together in California, Mia told Frank that she was anxious to star in a remake of the film *Johnny Belinda* for television. Producer David Susskind was initially against the idea of giving Mia the part. He told an interviewer, "She can't act, she's too thin, she's Frank Sinatra's wife, and she has the sex appeal of Spam." But Mia was able to overcome his objections and actually get the part.

During filming, Mia arrived on the set looking very badly beaten. Susskind said to her, "Mia dear, I don't think someone wants you to do this role."

Mia continued to work and never accused Sinatra of being anything more than a loving husband. According to a close friend, "Despite whatever problems they had, and the bad way Frank would treat her now and then, there was never any question as to the depth of Mia's love for her husband. She loved Frank, very deeply.

"That is why to this day, even though they have been split for over two decades, Mia has never publicly or privately uttered a bad word about him.

"Hard as it is to believe, and as difficult as he was, Mia loved being Mrs. Frank Sinatra.

"Frank also loved Mia very much. But he married her with the sincere hope that she would give full attention to just being Mrs. Frank Sinatra: when that didn't happen they started to have their problems."

Sinatra's daughter Nancy, in her 1985 biography *Frank Sinatra, My Father*, says that Mia and Sinatra were very much in love. When she asked Mia to recall the best times with her father, Nancy Sinatra reports that Mia wrote to her: "When I think of the time we were alone together (my favorite time), it sounds too sentimental . . crossword

puzzles . . . spaghetti sauce . . . TV in bed . . . our puppies
. . . walks . . . breakfasts . . . all those orange things . . .
his incredible sweetness . . . the purity of his feelings . . .
his smile.

"Looking back, I think that for us, our ages finally mat-
tered. I was too ill at ease with his remoteness and unable
to fathom his complexities. Though I knew how much he
needed it, given my real immaturity I could not . . . I was
not capable of being enough of a friend . . . however much
I wanted to be. We had a great amount of love between
us but we lacked understanding in everyday life as well as
of the major, deeper themes. Today he is still a part of
me. I think of him often and wish him the very best because
he deserves it and, of course, because I love him."

Veteran Hollywood reporter Vernon Scott, a longtime
observer of the couple, wrote in the *Ladies' Home Journal*
a few months after Mia and Frank were married, "Any
marriage is a gamble, but I think there is a good chance
this one will last. In a few years, Mia will be one of the
biggest stars in motion pictures. Undoubtedly, her career
has been and will be helped by the influence and luster of
the man that she married. But she was well on her way
before she met Sinatra, and she married him not to zoom
into orbit but because she loves him.

"Mia Farrow Sinatra is having the most wonderful life
any twenty-two-year-old has ever had. She is married to
a colorful, complex, gifted man whose every mood fascinates her. She has new homes, clothes, jewelry, servants,
pets, fans, and interests; private jet planes and helicopters
whisk her from place to place, and her movie career is just
blossoming. She is everything she ever wanted to be. What
woman could possible want more?"

Scott's prognostication about a long marriage would

prove to be incorrect. The dramatic upheavals in Mia's life didn't end with her marriage to Sinatra. While Mia had already done more living in her twenty-two years than most do in a lifetime, there was still much more for her to do, including her most profound professional experience. Living with the often devilish Sinatra was nothing compared to playing the mother of Satan's child, as Mia was about to do in one of her most important films, *Rosemary's Baby*.

CHAPTER 4

ROSEMARY'S BABY
AND MORE

$\mathcal{F}$EW films affect dramatically the lives of all their major participants. *Rosemary's Baby* did. Not only did the film fully establish Mia Farrow as a serious screen talent, it was the final straw in the breakup of her marriage to Frank Sinatra. The film also enabled Mia to meet the next man to play an important romantic role in her life.

But before any of this could happen, Mia, like any working actress, had to land the part. *Rosemary's Baby* was a best-selling novel by Ira Levin. The dark and eerie story of a naive woman who slowly comes to realize that her husband has tricked her into giving birth to the child of Satan captivated the nation. The hot topics of sex and the devil made the book a controversial thriller. Hollywood was anxious to make this film, and by 1967, when filming actually began, Hollywood executives felt that perhaps America was finally ready to see on the screen many of the highly controversial topics explored in the pages of the book.

Paramount Pictures acquired the rights to the book and hired noted director Roman Polanski to both write the screenplay and direct the film. Because the film was based on such a hot book, Paramount intended to spare no expense in casting the movie. Anyone that Polanski and the studio could agree on would be signed for the film.

The book's description of Rosemary called for a full-figured, well-rounded, all-American girl. Hovering around a hundred pounds, Mia certainly didn't fit the description.

Polanski interviewed dozens of actresses. Like many studios during this time, Paramount had many actresses under exclusive contract, and while the edict was out to get the best actress at any cost, Polanski knew that picking one of the women already under contract to Paramount would mean he might have more money for other aspects of the movie later. The Paramount contract players weren't good enough for Polanski, and he was ready to go out and interview the rest of the actresses in Hollywood if he had to.

Near the top of Polanski's list was actress Tuesday Weld, a friend of Polanski's then-girlfriend Sharon Tate. Polanski suggested Weld to Paramount, but she was rejected because the studio felt she didn't have enough marquee value for a movie of such importance.

Time was running short and Polanski needed to find someone, when Paramount production executive Bob Evans suggested Mia Farrow. In his autobiography, *Roman*, Polanski writes of first meeting Mia at the Daisy nightclub in Beverly Hills. He watched a few episodes of *Peyton Place* in advance of their meeting and was impressed with her work on the series. Polanski recalls, "Although Mia didn't fit Levin's description or my own mental image of Rosemary, Mia's acting ability was such that I hired her without a screen test."

Mia herself desperately wanted to leave *Peyton Place* and work in a truly important film. Based on preproduction plans and the incredible media interest the project generated before even a frame of film was shot, *Rosemary's Baby* was destined to be a blockbuster. Mia landed the role she needed. Through *Peyton Place* and the marriage to Sinatra, Mia had already achieved tremendous celebrity. Now she was looking for something more substantial to base her career on. With every film critic in the country eagerly awaiting the opening of the movie, if Mia could deliver, she could get the professional respect that she felt she needed. As she said, "This film meant a great deal to me both privately and professionally."

Polanski also struggled in his search for a leading man for the film to play the demonic husband Guy. Initially Polanski wanted superstar Robert Redford, but since he and Paramount were involved in a nasty legal battle, he wasn't seen as a reasonable choice. The director also considered actor Jack Nicholson, who lobbied heavily for the part. But both Polanski and Paramount felt that Nicholson wasn't well known enough to be the leading man in such a major motion picture. (Nicholson and Polanski eventually enjoyed great success together in the film *Chinatown*.)

Mia's leading man was finally chosen when Polanski and Paramount agreed upon actor and director John Cassavetes. The casting of Cassavetes made the making of *Rose-*

mary's Baby an even more dramatic experience. Mia and Polanski worked well together, but Cassavetes and Polanski fought bitterly.

Cassavetes thought that Polanski, among other things, was too interested in the macabre. "You just try to keep alive with Roman," he said, "or you go under. He is so obsessed with the bloody and the gruesome, behaving like a kid in a candy store."

During rehearsals and initial filming the contrast between the smooth working rapport between Roman and Mia versus the hysterics between Roman and John became apparent. Polanski was a tough director and a very autocratic one; he would ask his cast to perform a particular scene in a particular way, and that was exactly what he wanted done.

Noted Hollywood production designer Richard Sylbert worked on the film. He recalled that during preproduction and filming, "Making a movie during that time was like having a giant party, and Roman was the host and master of ceremonies. He was in top form. His own life was good. He was living with Sharon Tate and they were very happy, and with that security from his personal life, Roman was ready to face the Hollywood establishment head-on."

Polanski's first line of attack was his leading man. While Mia sat quietly waiting for the next take, Polanski would verbally rake Cassavetes over the coals for a particular performance. He taunted Cassavetes with critical comments about films that Cassavetes himself had made. Roman did whatever he could to create tension on the set, and his favorite device was fighting with Cassavetes. But the real fireworks on the set didn't come directly from a member of the production company. The true behind-the-scenes drama stemmed from the total collapse of Mia's marriage.

Sylbert, who became close to Mia during filming, said, "Mia Farrow is one very, very smart woman. She knew this film was something new for her and would launch her career in exciting new directions.

"Mia was a good choice for the part both on the surface and underneath. *Rosemary's Baby*, after all, was her first serious movie.

"The problem with Mia was with her marriage to Frank Sinatra, and the problems started to show up real soon."

Sylbert says that Frank was stunned by Mia's decision to accept the role in the film. "I can remember one dinner with Frank, where he would sit around and just tell stories of the old days. He would tell us stories about how he learned to hold his breath and how he learned perfect breath control for singing.

"But what he was most interested in talking about was what he wanted in his life after his divorce from Ava Gardner. What Frank said was that he wanted a wife who would stay home. Suddenly he finds himself with a new wife, and not only didn't she stay at home, she was taking a starring role in the most talked-about movie of the year."

Sylbert and others on the set confirm that Mia's acceptance of the role in *Rosemary's Baby* was the death knell for her marriage. "It was that clear a decision," said Sylbert. "Frank was in essence saying to Mia, 'You do this movie and our marriage is over.' But Frank underestimated Mia's great inner strength—she wasn't about to be bullied, certainly not by Frank. She went on to do the movie, and it clearly established her as a major film actress."

Mia's fine performance did not come without personal

and often painful sacrifice. A memorable scene in the film shows a dazed Rosemary crossing New York's Fifth Avenue in the middle of rush-hour traffic. Such a scene would normally be shot using stunt drivers and on a carefully controlled street or studio backlot. But with Polanski in the director's chair, such standard precautions were thrown aside. Mia recalls the scene vividly. "We didn't organize the traffic at all," she said. "We just did it. Roman said, 'Nobody's going to hit a pregnant lady, not on Fifth Avenue.' "

At Polanski's insistence, without any rehearsal, he virtually chased Mia across the crowded street while filming her with a small hand-held camera. The danger shown on-screen was no Hollywood creation—Mia barely got across the street without being hit or run down. After she finally made it across, Polanski laughed and told her that it was an excellent take and that he wouldn't ask her to do it again.

Another scene called for Mia to be inducted into a witches' coven; during the scene she was shoved and pushed and kicked and hit. The scene required over twenty takes before Polanski was satisfied. Mia never asked for a stunt double to be used.

In a scene with a doctor taking a blood sample, Mia insisted that a real sample be taken. She felt that by actually feeling the needle sting she would be able to add even more verisimilitude to the particular sequence. Polanski, thrilled with her realistic suggestion, brought in a trained medic to draw the blood on film.

In many ways the film was so realistic that years later some of Mia's fans still associate her directly with the picture. In a 1984 interview, Mia told film critic Roger Ebert,

"It's a funny thing, a lot of people still think that I live in the Dakota [the infamous New York apartment building where much of *Rosemary's Baby* was filmed, and where, later, John Lennon was shot to death].

"Usually movies don't make that much of an impression, but people to this day somehow assume that was my apartment."

Mia's hardships took place both on- and off-camera. Sinatra was furious with her for taking the part, and the results of their fighting became clear to all on the set. Cast and crew would look at Mia with concern. Her frail frame was victimized by the grueling shooting schedule and by what was happening to her at home with Sinatra.

One member of the production team recalls, "Frank's a hitter. There was some physical stuff going on between him and Mia, there is no question about that."

As filming continued, Frank turned up the pressure on Mia. He would phone the set, and when Mia would take his call on an in-studio line, those in the production could actually hear Frank's voice screaming while Mia just quietly held onto the phone.

Frank wanted Mia to walk off the set of the movie, as he had done with other films in the past. He wanted her to join him on the set of his movie *The Detective*, which was about to begin filming in New York. Sinatra even called top executives at Paramount to ask how much longer Polanski would require Mia for *Rosemary's Baby*. When Sinatra was told that Mia would continue to be needed on the set for a month or more, he responded with a threat that she would be leaving the set in two weeks whether the movie was finished or not.

Mia wasn't moving, though. She was still working on

some of the smaller details of the film. Songwriter Chris Komeda had penned a lullaby as a title theme for the film, and Polanksi auditioned successively more than six professional singers to hum the title tune. But he didn't think any of them made the tune haunting enough, so he asked Mia herself to perform the song. Mia explained, "I won out over your better Hollywood hummers. I think it could have been pretty popular, but I guess we've got enough singing Sinatras already."

The more Sinatra continued his clamor for Mia to walk off the film, the more she resisted. Richard Sylbert recalls, "Mia was determined to finish this movie. It was much too important to her to give up, for any other role, or for her marriage. Mia's choice was clear."

And Sinatra's retaliation was swift. A few weeks after she refused to leave the set, Mia was handed divorce papers right on the Paramount lot where *Rosemary's Baby* was filming. Despite the trauma of losing her husband, Mia never lost her professional composure and caused no delay in filming.

Mia shocked the Hollywood community by actually flying to Mexico during a day off from shooting and processing the divorce herself. She asked for no alimony or any of Sinatra's assets. Mia's quick action indicated that she was just as happy to be rid of Sinatra and wanted no financial ties to him.

According to one *Rosemary's Baby* executive, "Mia and Frank's divorce was quick and quiet; a complete opposite from the massive media coverage their marriage had generated. Mia could have dragged Frank through the mud and received a king's ransom in alimony, but she would have none of it. This was a closed chapter in her life and she wanted to get on with the business of living."

She also had to get on with the business of acting. A few weeks after *Rosemary's Baby* was edited, Mia arranged for private screenings for some of her friends. "I was terrified," she recalled. "I was really putting my head on the block and saying, 'There you are. That's what I can do.' "

Paramount Pictures needed no convincing of Mia's abilities. After seeing the final cut of the film they launched a massive advertising campaign. With the eerie theme line "Pray for Rosemary's Baby," publicity posters sprang up around the country. Dell Books released 1.5 million paperback copies of the novel, just in time for the film's premiere.

The advance goodwill on the film spilled over to many of the participants. Recalled Sylbert, "In those days, making a movie was just like having a big wonderful party. And after the party on the set was over, there would often be parties taking place all over town."

A particular social clique developed from *Rosemary's Baby*. The group included Mia, Polanski, Sylbert, film producer Mike Nichols, actor Anthony Perkins, and others. This celebratory group would often get together for dinner parties at each other's home. It was during one particular dinner party at Nichols's home, right after Mia and Frank's relationship was over, that Mia met André Previn.

Previn was an internationally known composer and conductor. He was arguably as important in the classical music world as Sinatra was in more popular music circles. He and his wife Dory were invited to the dinner party because he had done some movie scoring work for some of the guests. He and Mia spoke and were clearly charmed by each other, but Previn was married, and Mia was just recovering from her divorce. If there was any great romantic fire between the two, they kept it in check at the first meeting. But a year and a half later there would be other meetings, culminating in an explosive romance and marriage.

The overriding concern of most members of this clique was the fate of *Rosemary's Baby*, both with the critics and at the box office. Sylbert said, "We all knew that we had done something very, very special. But we didn't know what would happen when the film was actually released. All we could do was wait."

They didn't have to wait long. Within days of its release the film, and especially Mia, drew immediate raves. The *Hollywood Reporter* said, "Mia Farrow has made the role totally her own, turning the one-dimensional extremities of innocence, pain, and horror into a distinctively personal achievement. One of the best performances by a screen actress this year."

Richard Sylbert said, "The film was a hit, and a moneymaker; everyone was thrilled with the results." The thriller won great praise for Polanski, but he was quick to share the credit. He told *Look* magazine, "I have no doubt that I'm nuts, and Mia too. There are 127 varieties of nuts. She's 116 of them. That may be the reason she is so charming. I never had trouble with her. She's sensitive, she enjoys it, she has a neurotic quality good for Rosemary. Only the nuts are interesting people."

Mia's behavior took a decidedly bizarre turn after *Rosemary's Baby*. The twenty-two-year-old actress had already starred in a hit TV series, married one of the world's most famous men, and played the lead in a worldwide hit film. But despite all her achievements, Mia set out on a unique odyssey that would take her halfway around the world and put her in close contact with, among others, the Beatles. Mia Farrow, known to millions the world over, was now determined to find herself.

CHAPTER 5

MIA'S SEARCH

SPIRITUAL enrichment has always been important to Mia. When she was a child, John Farrow decreed that Mia was to be brought up in a strict Catholic home. The family went to church weekly, and religious holidays were rigidly observed.

Mia spent her entire childhood and adolescent years in the confines of a religious world. She attended only parochial schools from kindergarten through high school. But as Mia left the school yard for the film studio, it was impossible for her to find the comfort that she once had found in traditional religious practices.

Privately Mia began to question her inbred beliefs and begin to explore new spiritual alternatives. Her blind faith in Catholicism diminished, and by the time she took the un-Catholic step of divorcing Frank Sinatra, she had fallen away from the Church almost totally.

As was common among many entertainers in the late 1960s, Mia turned away from the practice of accepted Western religions. She instead became fascinated with mysticism, Eastern philosophy, astrology, and transcendental meditation. Her interest in TM continued to intensify as she ascended to even greater heights of stardom.

As she was basking in the warmth of the reviews of *Rosemary's Baby*, Mia wasn't busily looking for the next great script; instead she was hoping to find the next great truth. She began to study alternative philosophy. Mia said of Eastern philosophy, "It really is a mathematical formula for mind expansion. They've always said the kingdom of heaven is within—the trick is how you get there."

For an outsider looking in, Mia's current high standing in the Hollywood community, her marriage to Sinatra, and her considerable wealth would all seem to qualify as elements of Heaven on earth. But Mia simply wasn't satisfied with what she had found—she wanted more.

Her personal search for a higher truth became a personal trek, taking her thousands of miles from Hollywood to the Himalayas to study with the learned guru, the Maharishi Mahesh Yogi.

Mia's younger sister Prudence first introduced her to the teachings of the Maharishi, who started life as the son of a minor Indian government official. The Maharishi graduated from the University of Allahabad in the early 1940s and worked in a factory. In 1947, tired of the assembly line, and hearing a spiritual call, the Maharishi went to live in the hills, where he became a holy man.

Over a dozen years later he emerged from his hillside retreat and set up an organization, the International Med-

itation Society, to spread his message. The Maharishi remained virtually unknown to the Western world until the
Beatles discovered him through their interest in Indian
music.

The Beatles' endorsement introduced him to the rich
and famous. The Maharishi won many new disciples,
offering spiritual guidance to top entertainers including
the Beatles, the Rolling Stones, Donovan, and Shirley
MacLaine.

Mia and Prudence became close friends of the Beatles,
whom they met in London just before shooting began
on *Rosemary's Baby*. John, Paul, George, and Ringo liked
Mia and Prudence because the women refused to be awed
by them. A friend of Mia's said, "Sure the Beatles were
the biggest thing around, but after all, Mia had been
Mrs. Frank Sinatra, which put her almost on the same
footing."

The Beatles were especially enchanted with Mia's sister
Prudence, who was youthful and playful and didn't melt
around any of the Fab Four. The inspiration was right in
front of them, and shortly after spending some time with
her, the Beatles recorded "Dear Prudence," which went
on to become one of their classic songs on *The White Al-
bum*. The Beatles turned Prudence on to the Maharishi,
and she in turn turned Mia on to the guru.

In January 1968, Mia and Prudence flew to Boston to
hear the Indian speak to a group of Harvard law students.
It was then that Mia, so taken with the guru, decided to
go with Prudence to Rishikesh, India, for three months to
study with the Maharishi.

A publicist at Paramount Pictures released a news statement saying that the two were heading off to India. The

assignments were doled out quickly to reporters and photographers from around the world.

Once in India, Mia told reporters that she was going to
study with the Maharishi to "seek an inner peace." Mia
made an illuminating comparison between the life she had
just concluded with Frank Sinatra and the new life she was
hoping to begin based on the Maharishi's teachings, con-
cluding that the guru's students definitely had different
values than Sinatra's cronies. Mia said, "Life is important,
love is important. Giving is important. Here [in India] are
people who are like children, brought up with no false
standards.

"In America we are caught up in materialism, in all the
wrong values. I had been a part of a very tight, careful
scene, with bodyguards and all of it. When I went here I
was suddenly alone, really alone—but I felt less alone than
I've ever felt. I finally found a land where I wasn't a
stranger."

Mia certainly wasn't a stranger to the dozens of photographers carefully stationed in the small Indian village
with orders to get a photo of the American actress visiting
the mystical guru. Mia told reporters, "I'm spending two
hours a day meditating. I feel more at peace with myself.
I hope to emerge as a new person."

When questioned about her next career move Mia said,
"I'm leaving myself in the hands of God."

Mia had been in India for less than a month when she
heard that the Beatles were going to try to join her there.
Mia knew that the Beatles would bring with them even
more reporters and photographers and that the peaceful
purposes of her trip would be totally compromised. Mia
said that when she heard the Beatles were making their

way toward India, "I got into a panic. I had nightmares of armies of press invading. The press was already here in droves, in the trees, everywhere. It was bad enough when I was here by myself."

The aggressive Indian press did not endear themselves to Mia, who described them "as a hornet's nest that swarmed in the trees and ran on the ground like a pack of rats."

Mia decided to leave Rishikesh and explore other parts of the country. She embarked by herself on a three-week journey across India, hitchhiking aimlessly across the country looking for adventure.

Mia traveled by elephant, by truck, and by foot. Often she slept outdoors. She would pull her tentlike dress over her head and just sleep on the ground. "I was just kind of wandering," Mia said. "Hitchhiking on any kind of moving vehicle that would take me."

Among the many modes of transport Mia employed was a cart hauling sugar canes. Mia rode in the back, lost among the canes for seven hours. When she arrived at the Ganges River, a collapsed bridge blocked her passage. Undaunted, Mia slogged through the three feet of river water.

"I put all of my belongings on top of my head and stomped across the Ganges," Mia said. "I had my camera—a Kodak Instamatic, a book—Huxley's *Island*, one change of clothes and a Coke."

Mia's wild travels took her to a "funny restaurant" where she met some European hippies. "They were all colorfully dressed and I struck up a conversation with them. I asked them where they were off to and they told me they were headed to this magical place called Goa. It was supposed to be undiscovered paradise.

"I said, 'Maybe I'll see you there.' "

Mia then met and traveled with a group of friendly communal beggars who turned out to be a roving colony of lepers. "They were very gentle people," Mia said. However, she was so frightened after learning of their disease that, after parting company with them, she went back to a clearer part of the Ganges and scrubbed herself clean, as pilgrims have been doing for centuries.

The adventurous actress, who was now well out of the camera range of even the most ambitious lensmen, actually found her way to Goa and lived for a few nights on the picturesque beaches. She even phoned her brother Johnny from the beach area just to say hello. Finally, her thirst for adventure slaked, Mia left India.

In an interview with the *Ladies' Home Journal* after her trip, Mia said, "I may look unaware at times but the antennas are always out . . . searching for something big that is happening, that will add to or enhance my life and being.

"Here was a theory [the teachings of the Maharishi] that appealed to me. It seemed full of purpose and made good sense. I followed it, first out of curiosity, and a sense of something higher.

"I attacked with a terrific amount of hope. It hit me as true and that's incentive to pursue something."

But after reflecting upon her experience and after long discussions with other followers, Mia quickly soured on most of the teachings of the guru. She said, "Everyone made the mistake of trying to make a Christ figure out of him. He's a man. No religious man should try and become another pope-like figure. His edifices are bound to crumble."

Mia then told Phyllis Batelle of the Los Angeles *Herald Examiner*, "The tragedy is that he and those around him wanted to build another edifice. I followed the Maharishi because I couldn't find any other solace in the materialistic world—and it was a movie set. I closed my eyes and thought it would go away, but it didn't so I escaped."

Mia discovered that her escape to India only served to change her physical location. To seek the inner peace that she wanted, she was going to have to continue her search for self. However, she was quick to admit that the Maharishi gave her and thousands of other seekers one important tool: "The Maharishi did do one thing right. He put meditation in terms that the Western world could understand. That was important."

Mia said the benefits of regular meditation were many, including "instant enlightenment. Solutions to problems come in a flash. It's quite extraordinary. And then you can give more of yourself to people you love."

So enthusiastic were her feelings about the benefits of meditation that she even claimed, "Meditation should be taught in schools as a science of the mind. Everybody should meditate."

Mia's public pronouncements on what was still considered a "hippie, underground" subject brought her an unusual amount of public scorn. Because of her activities, many popular gossip columnists ran a series of unflattering items about Mia. Comments focused on her style of dress, which was called "flower-childish" and "genderless."

Public opinion also seemed to be running against Mia following her divorce from Sinatra and her return from India. A widely published quote that appeared in newspapers all over America came from a New York City cab driver, who responded to a reporter's question of what he thought of Mia Farrow. "Hell," he replied. "The next thing you know, she'll be practicing voodoo."

Mia realized that the press was having a field day with

her flaky image, and it troubled her. She said, "Ten thousand people march to get a paragraph in a paper. But I get pages—an inane actress girl talking about her great ideas on life. It bothers me, it offends me."

Still Mia was eager to tell reporters about any new psychic discovery. Upon returning from India, Mia resumed her friendship with actress Ruth Gordon, a costar from *Rosemary's Baby*. With Gordon, Mia came to believe that when someone told her something exciting the information she was given could be transformed into what Mia called a "psychic energizer," which would have an almost miraculously uplifting quality.

Mia told Batelle of the *Herald Examiner*, "Ruth Gordon, who is one of my best friends, will call and will tell me something terrific on the phone.

"Suddenly the circles under my eyes disappear and I can go out all night. Just keep some terrific, exciting information in mind, and impart it to somebody and zap! The night is made. Groovy."

Another of Mia's best friends, and one who had a profound spiritual influence on her life, was artist Salvador Dali. After their meeting in New York, Mia and the artist had kept in regular touch, even as she became a more and more important film star. Back in the States, Mia complained to Dali that her life had fallen into a bit of a rut. The painter suggested that Mia switch her shoes, wearing each of them on the wrong foot for a couple of days.

Mia told Dali a few days later that the experiment provided her with unique and twisted perceptions. Dali asked her if her life was in a rut any longer, and Mia happily said, "No." A proud Dali told her that the experiment had worked.

Mia's trip to India, though unsuccessful in helping to

find a greater sense of inner peace, did give her a new personal style for both her wardrobe and her New York City apartment. Writer John Hallowell observed that her apartment "had been transformed into India with great crimson carpets and statues of elephants and crying Indian music. The most interesting real object was a pocket kaleidoscope of the sea. Mia said, 'The sea—it's all that I have at the moment.' She then rushed out to point out the window at the East River. She added: 'That too, I have that.' "

Mia was apparently no closer to finding her true spiritual self; though she lived in New York, she made many trips to England. And during a visit in London, she renewed her friendship with André Previn. Soon the relationship between Previn and Mia would take an unexpected turn, leaving Mia to suffer through the worst possible publicity and to enjoy the greatest imaginable romance—both at the same time. Mia was also about to embark on another chapter of her life—one that she would find to be the most important and satisfying of all. Mia was soon going to become a mother.

A striking beauty with haunting eyes, Mia was just twenty-two years old when she captured the hearts of America with her sensitive portrayal of the troubled Allison MacKenzie on the first nighttime T.V. drama, *Peyton Place*, and won the heart of perhaps the most sought-after man in the world, Frank Sinatra. *Levin/Camera Press/Photo Trends*

As a toddler, Mia and her father, noted film director and writer John Farrow, make a birthday wish for the future. In later years, their opinions of just what that future would be differed dramatically. The elder Farrow, who had seen his share of the seamier side of Hollywood, did not want his daughter to become an actress. John Farrow died before Mia reached her first great professional success. *Neal Peters Collection*

The Farrow family celebrates the baptism of Mia's youngest sister Tisa in 1951. Pictured are John Farrow, Prudence, John, Jr., Mia (arrow), Patrick, Stephanie, Maureen O'Sullivan, and Michael. The Farrows were a very religious family and neighbors recall seeing all of them in church every Sunday. The family was shattered by Michael's death in a plane crash eight years later. *Pictorial Parade Inc.*

Mia and her mother Maureen O'Sullivan shake hands for the cameras over lunch. Mia has followed her mother's footsteps as both an actress and a mother to a large family. But unlike Maureen, who chose to put her career on hold while raising her family, Mia has been able to balance the demands of both career and motherhood. The two have remained very close and Maureen visits with her daughter and many grandchildren often. Maureen also enjoys a friendship with Woody Allen, who cast her in his film *Hannah and Her Sisters*. She played Mia's mother. *Phototeque*

The ABC nighttime drama *Peyton Place* was incredibly popular and Mia was offered what was then considered a fortune, an annual salary over $100,000 to remain with the show once her contract expired in early 1966. Instead, she left to marry Frank Sinatra. Here she is pictured with costars Barbara Parkins, who played socialite Betty Anderson, and Ryan O'Neal as handsome Rodney Harrington. *Neal Peters Collection*

Mr. and Mrs. Frank Sinatra. She was twenty-two, he was fifty. When they married on July 19, 1966, radio and television stations interrupted regular programming for special bulletins on the surprise four-minute Las Vegas ceremony. Less than two years later, Mia and Frank divorced. *Pictorial Parade Inc.*

Ten years after Mia and Frank were divorced, cameramen caught a unique picture of Mia and another former Mrs. Frank Sinatra, actress Ava Gardner. While smiling happily here, when first learning of the relationship between her former husband and Mia, Gardner was widely reported as saying, "I always knew that Frank would end up in bed with a boy." *Ron Galella*

In what is perhaps her most acclaimed film performance, Mia portrayed the young wife deceived into carrying the child of the devil in *Rosemary's Baby*. Mia won the role over many other actresses after winning the respect of noted director Roman Polanski. *Neal Peters Collection*

In August of 1968, Mia returns from her search for self-meaning in India. After a brief visit with Guru Maharishi Yogi, Mia left his compound prior to the arrival of the Beatles for fear that she would be harassed by the hordes of international press covering the band. Instead Mia embarked on a three-week trip, hitchhiking alone across India. Upon arrival in England, Mia said, "It has been the most rejuvenating experience of my life. I feel I am better equipped to face my problems." *Pictorial Parade Inc.*

Only a few short years after her return from India, Mia's life had changed completely. As André Previn's third wife, Mia enjoyed the quiet life of wife and mother in the English countryside. After giving birth to twins Matthew and Sascha, the Previns adopted Lark Song, pictured here, an orphan from Vietnam. *Pictorial Parade Inc.*

In July of 1974, Mia and André are pictured here with their growing family. Twins Matthew and Sascha hold their parents hands, while Mia holds their newborn baby Fletcher, and André holds Lark. Mia and André would adopt two more children, Summer Song and Soon-Yi, before the break-up of their marriage in 1979. *Photo Trends*

Mia Farrow and her romantic companion since 1980, film director/writer Woody Allen. Allen has befriended all of Mia's children, and together with Mia, adopted a baby, Dylan, in 1985. Despite his public persona as a reclusive bachelor, Mia and Woody are regularly seen all over New York City. *Smeal/Gallella Ltd.*

Mia has never generated more laughter than in her role as gangster moll Tina Vitale, opposite Woody as the beleaguered talent agent, in *Broadway Danny Rose* in 1984. To prepare for the role, Mia listened carefully to tape-recorded conversations of heavily accented Brooklyn natives. *Phototeque*

A very pregnant Mia, just weeks before the birth of her and Woody Allen's child. Mia gave birth to a boy, Satchel O'Sullivan Farrow in late 1987. Satchel is Farrow's ninth child, and fifty-seven-year-old Woody Allen's first naturally fathered baby. At forty-two, Mia Farrow has experienced more in the first half of her life than most people experience in an entire lifetime. *Ron Galella*

CHAPTER 6

FROM MISTRESS
TO MOTHER

BACK in London, after her trip to India, Mia was hoping to continue her film career after the runaway success of *Rosemary's Baby*. Mia took an active role in reclaiming her career. She made sure she was at all the right parties and was seen with all the right people. Recalled a close friend, "Mia had to show the world she wanted to work again, that she wasn't as interested in the counterculture as she was in getting a new movie role."

Meanwhile, noted composer and musical director André Previn was also in London. Previn, who along with his wife Dory had composed the music for dozens of Hollywood films including *Irma la Douce* and *Goodbye Charlie*, was also currently employed as the conductor for the Houston Symphony.

In their comprehensive work *André Previn: A Biography*, writers Martin Bookspan and Ross Yockey detail Mia and Previn's meeting in London in 1967. Previn was brought to a show-business party by his brother, who worked in the film industry in England. "It was absolutely the epitome of a bullshit publicity party," Previn said. "Hundreds of people were milling around pretending undying love to one another whereas in truth they either loathed each other or hadn't seen each other in twenty years and would knife each other in the back if given an opportunity. . . . I began to feel very hemmed in and I didn't feel like standing around in that room any longer so I went to breathe some air on the sidewalk. I turned around and there she was. Mia Farrow."

This was not the first meeting between Mia and Previn, who is sixteen years her senior. When Mia was just nineteen and in Hollywood, her godfather, director George Cukor, introduced her to Previn when they were all together on the 20th Century-Fox lot. Additionally, Mia, as Mrs. Frank Sinatra, ran into Previn during various events in and around Hollywood. At that time Previn was married to Dory. In her autobiography, *Bog-Trotter*, Dory Previn recalled meeting Mia for the first time in California. "Mia said, 'Everyone I love, loves you. Everyone I love, loves you both. So I must introduce myself to you.' She walked across a long patio just to meet us. The natural surroundings conspired to enhance the luminous youth. The background was lit by banks of white daisies. . . . Mia's skin was translucent as though she were still wrapped in the gauze of her placenta. The voice had been gently buffed by good schools and privilege. . . . No pig in the parlor she. . . . This was lace-curtain Hollywood. She was second-generation MGM. And the newly famed waif wanted to be our friend." André Previn recalls, "I said hello to her and she remembered me. I asked her why she was leaving the party so early and she said because she couldn't stand it in there. I said, 'Well, that's interesting because I can't stand it either. How about going out to have dinner? She agreed, so we went out to dinner."

This dinner was far more successful than a dinner André had had with Mia some time earlier. Then, André and Dory, Mia and director Mike Nichols all went out. Dory Previn sensed and was concerned by a particular emotional attachment between her husband and Mia, but she thought it was based on dislike. She wrote of that ill-fated evening, "Mia said to Mike that she wanted to play Peter Pan. For in fact, she said, she had been to never-never land many times. 'You've been to no such place Mia,' my husband said to her. 'If you say anything so stupid again, I'll throw you out of the car!' I wondered why she annoyed him. And I was secretly glad. It had become difficult for a woman forty and more to see a girl much less than twenty-four in any guise other than perfect. And that perfection was beginning to threaten."

Dory Previn's sense of apprehension proved all too correct. Her husband's solo dinner date with Mia in London quickly blossomed into an all-out romance. Because of Mia's newly divorced status, coupled with the fact that Previn was a married man, the press had a field day.

Mia, still recovering from her marriage to the brooding Sinatra, was charmed by the refined manners and intellectual nature of the celebrated musical genius. She was happy in love, but the incredible press attention she and Previn generated upset her. "The last thing I want to be is someone's breakfast news," said Mia. "If I seem to be running, it's because I'm pursued."

But Mia was not the only one feeling offended. According to English music journalist Denise Hall, pressure from Previn's employers mounted. The board of directors of the Houston Symphony Orchestra, tired of reading about their conductor in the gossip column, and knowing that their conservative Texas patrons would not approve of their donations' supporting an orchestra headed by a man carrying on a public affair while married, believed that Previn had to either get his house in order or leave. A Houston area journalist wrote, "The Houston Board of Directors objected to his pop-lifestyle, exemplified by his headline-capturing romance with actress Mia Farrow."

Writers Bookspan and Yockey also contend that Previn's relationship with the Houston Symphony was compromised by artistic differences. Still, Previn's ultimate departure from the Houston Symphony did not result in any employment problems for him. Before severing all ties with the Houston Symphony he was offered the considerably more prestigious position of conducting the noted London Symphony Orchestra (LSO). The ambitious conductor actually served as principal conductor for both symphonies for a while, which resulted in an incredibly busy schedule, including over a dozen trips between the two orchestras. That pace of travel was another factor in the deterioration of Previn's marriage to Dory. For the-then Mrs. Previn had a fear of flying.

During 1969, Mia and Previn became more and more seriously involved. When Mia costarred with Dustin Hoffman in the film *John and Mary*, which was shooting in New York, she too traveled regularly across the Atlantic to spend time with Previn in London. During that same year Dory Previn received an Academy Award nomination for the song "Come Saturday Morning," from the film *The Sterile Cuckoo*. Dory Previn, who had suffered recurring bouts of mental illness both before and during her marriage to André Previn, was hospitalized in Los Angeles when the nomination was announced. There are conflicting versions as to what happened next.

Dory Previn writes that she received a letter of congratulation from her husband in the hospital. "At the end of the letter he asked me for a divorce. In reply to the request for the divorce I said yes." Bookspan and Yockey contend that André Previn "emotionally denies this. He insists that any words about separation were spoken face-to-face." Whatever the truth, André Previn filed for divorce in the latter half of 1969.

To add salt to her wounds, Dory writes that shortly after she learned of the divorce proceedings she was phoned by an unnamed gossip columnist who told her that Mia was pregnant with Previn's child.

In a dramatic example of Dory's impaired mental condition, Bookspan and Yockey report that after the divorce proceedings were begun, "Dory secured a pass from the hospital to attend a recording session. Instead she boarded a plane for London. First she telephoned André from the airport and asked him to meet her at Heathrow. . . . But Dory did not disembark in London."

It was later discovered that Dory "had been taken off the plane before it ever left the ground in Los Angeles. She had stood up in her seat screaming as the Pan-Am jet taxied to the runway. Dory then had ripped off most of her clothes and had run barebreasted down the aisle of the plane, shouting threats at a priest who happened to be on board. The plane stopped and an ambulance was called to take Dory to Culver City Hospital. It was the finish of her efforts to save the marriage. André, of course, had stopped trying long before.''

.With Mia actually pregnant by Previn, Dory and André agreed to try to formalize a divorce agreement. Years later Dory was able to understand what happened to her marriage. She wondered in *Bog-Trotter* why Previn had stayed married to her as long as he had. Dory wrote, "He divorced me. He had the better grounds. His indiscretion was less than mine. He left me for another woman long after I deserted him for another reality."

André Previn, reflecting on the divorce, said, "Dory now realizes in retrospect that no matter how painful it was for her at the time, it was to our mutual benefit to break up. It was our mutual salvation."

While the years appear to have diminished the harsh feelings between Dory and André, at the time of the divorce Dory made things as difficult as possible for André and Mia. Dory believed that Mia had become pregnant as part of a secret plan to steal her husband away from her. Dory was able to get back at Mia in a very public forum, pop music. Dory wrote and recorded a song called "Beware of Young Girls" that became an international hit. The lyrics about a young woman who covets an older woman's husband spoke so directly to Mia that they stuck her like thousands of sharp pins.

Dory told the *Los Angeles Times*, "It wasn't written as a vendetta. I hope people won't dwell on macabre personal relationships. Of course, there were personal reasons involved when I wrote it, but I'd like it to be judged as the statement of a universal female fear. Some of my friends have been through the same thing."

Richard Sylbert, a keen observer of Hollywood during

this time, agrees with Dory Previn when she says she was not alone. "The end of the 1960s was a terrible time for first wives in the entertainment business," he said. "First wives absolutely got slaughtered. They fell like logs. So even though Mia wasn't the only younger woman getting a newly divorced husband, she was certainly among the most public, and it generated a lot of resentment."

For her part, Mia denied that she stole Previn away from Dory. In an interview with entertainment writer Mel Gussow, Mia said, "I became involved with André after my marriage and his marriage had disintegrated. Then Dory wrote that tasteless song—but it simply wasn't true."

In a somewhat disjointed postscript to her version of events surrounding the song, Dory Previn wrote in *Bog-Trotter*, "Mia called 'Beware of Young Girls' tasteless. I was indignant she chose to discuss me and disappointed she hadn't said more. The critique was included in a long myth of how and when she met my husband. Myths don't bother me; we all make up things.

"She rates the song as without value? Yes I suppose it is. God knows I have not made a dime from it. . . . now she says the song is blameless. Ah well, if she means the song is tactless, out-of-touch, untaxing, valueless and blameless, then I agree with her. It is tasteless."

Pained by the song and continued press coverage, a very pregnant Mia set up house with André in a less than luxurious flat in Belgravia. Friends began to wonder why Mia, with no assurance that André would ever become free, decided to continue the pregnancy. A friend told *Parade* magazine. "How easy it would be for Mia to get an abortion here, rather than giving birth out of wedlock, but Mia simply wouldn't do it."

As one reporter wrote, "It was a difficult period for the

lovers as they waited for the birth of the child and the freedom to marry. They weren't sure which would happen first." The press began a daily vigil outside their flat, and photographers would hide out, hoping to catch a picture of the still unmarried couple with child. Mia recalled, "We would go to the market, and there would be people behind us with cameras. It was unbelievable."

According to British journalist Denise Hall, "Mia and André were living under a microscope and it was especially difficult for André. To some degree Mia had already survived her first media baptism of fire with Frank Sinatra. But this was all too much for the dignified conductor.

"On one particular day he stared out of the window of the flat and was shocked to discover a cameraman with a large telephoto lens focusing right in on him. Clearly things had gotten out of hand and André mused to Mia that there must be some particular way to deal with the press.

"At Mia's suggestion, André called a chap who was with a public relations firm and sought out his advice. André's friend suggested that there was no way to beat off a hungry press, and that he and Mia were going to have to come out of hiding in some way.

"André understood the general message and decided to invite a particular photographer into the house. He allowed the lensman to take all the pictures he wanted to. Photos of him and Mia, of Mia's enlarged middle, of the flat, of the happy couple together.

"It was more than a $50,000 day for the particular photographer who sold the pictures around England and around the world. The tactic was quite successful; once the flood of photographs was released, the press retreated."

As Previn himself recalls, "We were prisoners. We simply stayed behind closed doors. Then the photos appeared, and it all eased up considerably."

In early 1970, Mia's life changed forever with the birth of her fraternal male twins Matthew and Sascha. As Mia entered motherhood she finally found in her children the sense of self she had always been searching for. Motherhood to Mia proved to be her most important role of all.

After months of trouble, other good news followed the birth of the twins. The divorce from Dory finally came through, and on September 10, 1970, Mia and André were married, in a small and quiet ceremony. No longer "notorious news," the Previns moved to a converted sixteenth-century tavern and inn called the Haven, located in Surrey, some twenty-five miles from London.

The house was surrounded by woods and streams. Inside the home, great attention had been paid to special interior features. Half-moon-shaped carvings were in each doorway, their original purpose being so that beer barrels could be easily rolled in. André and Mia carefully attended to each of the rooms in the house. André's study featured a piano for composing, and in it were photographs of the family and the surrounding area taken by Mia. The children's room was also a delight, painted in blues and yellow, and filled with many toys that Mia herself had made.

Describing the home Mia said, "You have to duck if you're over 5'10". Deer come to our window. We have a chicken and a goat. It's like Thomas Hardy country; the nearest village is a mile away. You can walk all day at the back of the house and see only woods." Mia frequently treated the family to picnics in the seemingly never ending backyard. Also in the woods was an original train caboose that served as a ground-level "tree house" for the youngsters.

Previn told *People* magazine, "Nobody ever bothers us." Previn went on to describe the family's idyllic country existence, which included Mia doing her own patchwork quilting and entertaining the twins with music and puppet shows. One of Mia and the children's favorite private shows was *Peter and the Wolf.* Said Previn, "They get the music and their mother's voice, all in one."

Mel Gussow reported that Previn used to tease his wife by displaying a book with a fake book jacket around it. He told Mia that he was working on a special book entitled *All I Know About Mia Farrow by André Previn.* Mia was shocked when Previn first told her about it, then relieved when she learned he was just kidding.

While motherhood was Mia's first and foremost concern, she was able to work on occasion, appearing in the films *See No Evil* and *The Public Eye.*

In 1971 Mia starred in a television movie, *Goodbye Raggedy Ann*, along with actor Hal Holbrook. Jack Sher, who wrote and produced the film, recalled, "Against the advice of her talent agent, Mia did *Goodbye Raggedy Ann*, simply because she fell in love with the script.

"Mia was getting very little money for the project, considering she was a feature film star by then. It was nowhere near what she was getting for feature films. When I first presented the project to her agent the first thing he asked was: 'How much do you want to pay her for this?' All he was interested in was the money. When I told him what we could pay, he responded, 'Mia wouldn't even read it for that kind of money.'

"Her agent wouldn't show it to her so we had to smuggle it to her behind her agent's back. The executive producer Phillip Barry called a friend at CBS who knew André

Previn, and Previn was able to get the script from us and give it to Mia.

"What I admire most about Mia is her artistic integrity. She insisted that no changes be made in the screenplay. In one scene the network censors wanted to cut because they thought the scene had certain sexual implications. It did not. The scene called for Mia to take a shower at a male friend's apartment. By today's standards it would be harmless. The network was quite serious about editing the scene out, and Mia called the head of the network and said that she would walk right off the set and go back to England if they dared cut a frame of that scene. The network backed down. Mia gave a great performance. She's a very sensitive actress. On the last day of production Mia signed a script for me. She wrote, 'Thank you Jack for all the words and for some of the nicest times in my whole life.' She signed it, 'Love Always, Mia.'

"I have worked with a lot of actresses, and Mia is certainly one of the very best. Both in front of the camera and in real life. She's wonderful."

Mia returned to England from the California film site determined to start working in the theater. During her marriage to Sinatra, Mia said to a reporter, "If I hadn't married Frank, I would probably be doing English repertory theater right now." While married to Previn, she was able to follow through on her wish. In an effort to strengthen her basic acting skills, Mia took to the British boards. In 1972 she made her British theatrical debut in the title role of J. M. Barrie's *Mary Rose*, in Manchester. André was more anxious than she was on opening night. He said, "She hadn't been onstage for so many years, I wondered whether her voice could be heard. . . . she could be heard to Yankee Stadium without a microphone." Soon after Mia also joined the prestigious Royal Shakespeare Company in London and made her debut in the title role of Harley Granville-Barker's play *The Marrying of Ann Leete*.

Insecure in her acting ability, Mia quivered at the prospect of working alongside such accomplished talents as Richard Pasco and Paul Rogers.

"I was frightened and allowed to be," says Mia. "I'd have been a fool not to. It's due to respect, respect for the company and respect for the other actors in the play."

Mia did, however, go on to win her fellow actors' admiration in that play and other Royal Shakespeare Company productions including Chekhov's *Ivanov, Zykovs*, and *The Three Sisters*, and Tom Stoppard and Garcia Lorca's *House of Bernarda Alba*.

"I took enormous satisfaction from that work," Mia said. "Bringing to life the words of a great dramatist . . . that's marvelous."

Fellow Royal Shakespeare Company member Ian Richardson said of Mia, "She was a very frightened little bird when she came to the RSC. But it was inconceivable that she could have joined in a minor capacity. She had to jump in the deep end."

Added RSC director David Jones, "There was absolutely no trace of 'film star' in her behavior. She just drinks up every direction you give her. She makes life easy for a director. She has an immense emotional truthfulness, a quality of sincerity. In performance she is fresh each time. She plays in the present tense."

Previn, in addition to supporting his wife's theater career, also appeared to have some other interests as well.

While touring with the London Symphony Orchestra, he befriended an attractive music critic, Gillian Widdicombe. Her early reviews of Previn were quite critical, calling him "the biggest publicity magnet since Beecham." She called his conducting technique "a kind of paddle." She compared him to a traffic cop, writing, "Previn's traffic doesn't always obey his signals."

But as the months passed and the two became friendly, the reviews suddenly became quite enthusiastic. Among them: "Previn fashions the dynamic detail with almost fastidious care."

The London gossip columnists went wild. Widdicombe added fuel to the fire by describing Mia in one of her reviews: "Previn's unusual wife who occasionally comes to concerts."

On several occasions Mia and Gillian showed up together at LSO events. Bookspan and Yockey write, "One source close to the LSO said, 'It was a rather bizarre situation, with his wife and his girlfriend in the hall at the same time. To everyone's relief they avoided each other.' "

For the first time in Mia's adult life, she exhibited a streak of jealousy. She did all that she could to suppress what she thought were negative and destructive feelings, but the constant irritation of hearing about her husband and Gillian proved to be too much. At one particular concert there was a confrontation between the two women. Mia was somehow placed in a seat directly behind Gillian's regular reserved seat. Throughout the concert, as Bookspan and Yockey describe it, she "slumped down in her seat so that she could dig her knees into Gillian's seatback, rocking forward to minimize Gillian's chances of enjoying the concert."

Added journalist Denise Hall: "First Mia and Gillian play pushy during the concert, and then later they have a great verbal free-for-all backstage.

"While Previn was locked away in his dressing room, the two women in his life were fighting over who should go in to see him. It was very bizarre. But Mia, who never had solid proof of what was said to go on between Gillian and André, decided to let the matter go. She never pressed André on his relationship with Gillian. Shortly after that particular concert, when André was gone for weeks during an LSO tour of the Soviet Union, Gillian covered the tour for her newspaper. The rumors again started flying, but Mia, with two babies at home and having no desire to uproot her beloved children and cast off the marriage, chose to let it go. She chose her love for Previn over any suspicions she may have had. Years later the clamor of the rumors about Andre's infidelity became too much for Mia to ignore. But by that time, the size of her family had more than doubled."

Although Mia was given many film offers in America, she had no interest in leaving the English countryside and her children. The Royal Shakespeare Company kept her occupied and expanded her acting abilities. "It was a wonderful experience for me," Mia recalled. "I could be at home with the children for most of the day, and then a car would come for me around four in the afternoon and I would go to the theater. I would be home early enough in the evening to look in on the children, before I myself went to bed. I was able to do some of the most challenging acting ever, and yet I never felt I compromised my obligations to the children."

Mia told writer M. George Haddad, "I try to be with my children as much as possible. Growing up is so difficult.

It's sometimes a trauma trying to find out who you are, what makes you different and in your own mind a little more special than all those little ant-humans you see when you're on the top story of a tall building. And it's especially difficult when you have one or more famous parents.

"My real childhood is my children's childhood; that's the one I can do something about."

Mia had made her own personal charge clear. Her life was her children, and she was very happy with her lot. Acting would continue to be somewhat incidental to Mia until 1973, when she would be drawn to star opposite Robert Redford in a film that was both heralded and reviled: *The Great Gatsby*.

CHAPTER 7
DAISY

*M*IA'S career had been relatively quiet as she concentrated on her domestic life as wife and mother. But *The Great Gatsby*, one of the most heavily promoted movies of all time, thrust her back into the limelight. Labeled by some critics one of the greatest blendings of art and commerce, *Gatsby* was both one giant movie and one giant commercial. Mia, despite her best efforts, became part of both.

Ironically, one of Mia's most important screen appearances, her role as Daisy in the film based on the classic F. Scott Fitzgerald novel, was a case of last-minute casting, similar to her casting in *Rosemary's Baby*. Mia got the part after careful consideration was given to other actresses. Mia actively lobbied for the role, which was originally intended for actress Ali McGraw of *Love Story* fame.

McGraw was married to Paramount production executive Robert Evans, a driving force behind *Rosemary's Baby* and a popular and powerful producer. According to Judy Lardner, who also worked at Paramount at the time, "The original idea of making a film of *The Great Gatsby* was Bob's. He wanted to give the role of Daisy to Ali as a present.

"Bob's only interest in doing *Gatsby* at the start was so that Ali would have the part she had always wanted."

Evans had intimated to friends that it was McGraw who first drew his attention to the Fitzgerald novel and convinced him that it would be an excellent vehicle for her.

Evans brought in noted producer David Merrick to help him obtain the rights to the project. Evans told Merrick in a conversation that was widely repeated throughout preproduction of the film, "I want to do this one for Ali."

It took Evans and Merrick over eighteen months of complicated negotiations with Fitzgerald's estate to secure the rights to the novel. Paramount paid a large upfront fee of $350,000, plus the usual promise of a percentage of future profits. Once the rights to the book were secured, Evans and Merrick looked over a long list of possible writers. Truman Capote tried his hand at a version, but it was rejected by Evans and Merrick, who turned to top director Francis Ford Coppola.

Coppola was also well regarded as a screenwriter and a script doctor, and he was known to work quickly. Evans was anxious to get the movie underway as fast as possible. He had been trying for so long to deliver this particular present to his wife that he didn't want to have to wait any longer than absolutely necessary.

Coppola came through with an acceptable version of the script in just three weeks, and Evans was thrilled. All Evans had to do now was find a director, and the rest of the cast to join with Ali. But much to Evans's surprise and brutal disappointment, the very mention of casting Ali as Daisy brought shudders from everyone he spoke to.

As Lardner recalled, "McGraw became well known for her work in *Love Story*, but her reputation as an actress was not good. She had been critically savaged for other work, and the feeling in much of the Hollywood community was that her beauty far outweighed any possible talent that she might have. Mia's reputation, on the other hand, was always that her professional abilities were far superior to her natural gifts, and that she could always work as an actress, if not as a model. But Evans wasn't even thinking of Mia, not yet anyway."

Evans was still obsessed with the idea that the role of Daisy in *Gatsby* was for Ali only, and that was that. A trio of top directors—Peter Bogdanovich, Arthur Penn, and Mike Nichols—were approached, but all declined the project because of Evans's insistence on casting McGraw.

Evans's problems went beyond finding a director: he couldn't find a leading man who would work with her, either. Warren Beatty said he could consider the project only if he could select his costar, and Jack Nicholson had no desire to share the marquee with McGraw.

Evans's biggest difficulty was actually with another actor, Steve McQueen. While Evans was busily trying to get *Gatsby* going for his wife, she and McQueen, working on another picture, *The Getaway*, had fallen in love and were carrying on an affair.

Shortly before Evans was about to find a director and a star who would work with McGraw, she filed for divorce, and the extent of her relationship with McQueen became public knowledge.

As Lardner recalls, "It was a terrible thing for Bob. Everyone in the world knew about Steve and Ali but him, and here he was trying to bust his hump so that she could be the star of this movie. Then when she filed for divorce, he couldn't go back to the leading men and the directors he had already decided against."

Evans had to save the project. He hired Robert Redford to play Gatsby and director Jack Clayton to film the project. Still, no lead actress had been selected. While Evans gave screen tests to Katherine Ross, Candice Bergen, Faye Dunaway, and others, he received an interesting piece of mail from the other side of the Atlantic.

Evans recalled, "When we were in the final throes of casting for *Great Gatsby* I got a note from Mia, and in the envelope was a small daisy. In a handwritten note to me, Mia wrote the simple sentence, 'Dear Robert, May I be your Daisy?'

"After all the initial start-up problems we had had, I was absolutely enchanted. Mia brought a mystical quality, there was just something about her that made her so very interesting to look at. And I knew that she wouldn't be trouble. The director Clayton agreed, and Mia was on the set in just a few weeks' time."

While the actual production had terrible trouble getting on its way, the publicity machine behind *The Great Gatsby* had been running at full force. There was such an incredible amount of hype behind this project that Mia, who had somewhat faded from the American scene after the publicity of her marriage to André Previn had subsided, was again brought to the forefront of American attention.

According to Smith, "The press people at Paramount

were determined to make this the biggest movie ever, and to do that meant making Robert Redford and Mia Farrow the most famous actor and actress around. The offset machines were running around the clock, churning out material on the two of them. Paramount made sure that every movie critic in America would know more about *The Great Gatsby* than they had ever known about any other film, and this was still months before the actual movie was ready to be screened."

The movie was shot on location in Newport, Rhode Island, and at the Pinewood studios near London. Mia was thrilled to be back before the cameras, especially in a project of such significance. She said, "Who wouldn't jump at a chance to do a huge and prestigious project like *Gatsby*? We're all children at heart and I love dressing up—those '20s clothes alone in my opinion justified seeing *Gatsby* and acting in it."

Paramount marketing executives agreed with Mia that the look of the film, including the clothes, the hairstyles, and more, were so important that all America might join the *Gatsby* bandwagon. Paramount executive Frank Yablans said, "There has never been a promotional campaign like this before."

In a unique and unprecedented marketing strategy, Paramount lined up four major corporate sponsors for *The Great Gatsby*. Each company was able to tie in its products to the film, and each company advertised to the hilt, drawing more attention to the project and to Mia. America was blitzed by ads from Ballantine's scotch ("Gatsby's Parties . . . Ballantine's was there"), Glemby International Hair Salons ("The Gatsby Cut"), Robert Bruce men's clothing ("The Gatsby Look"), and DuPont cookware, which had developed a special line of "Gatsby" white cooking pots and pans.

Women's Wear Daily featured "The Gatsy Look" as noted designer Kenzo Takada displayed 1920s tennis wear in an important Paris fashion show, and Paramount produced a free thirty-minute television special on the making of *The Great Gatsby*. As one Paramount executive put it, "The idea is to 'Gatsbyize' the entire country, and Mia was part of that 'Gatsbyization.'"

Frances Scott Fitzgerald Smith, a journalist and the only child of Zelda and F. Scott Fitzgerald, visited the *Gatsby* set during production. She observed, "When I first saw Mia on the set I thought she was ravishing, just breathtaking. The New England summer sun was hitting her face under this chiffon lilac hat and she looked just like my father's Daisy should look." Smith's remarks were reprinted many times as part of the promotional push.

In the midst of all the publicity, Mia had some unexpected news. Just a few weeks into filming, she discovered she was pregnant with her third child. Mia was thrilled with her condition but had to cope with the standard problems of morning sickness and exhaustion. Wardrobe crews had to make many adjustments to the lavish and detailed costumes that she wore. Because of her physical condition and some limitations in the script, Mia found it difficult playing the role of Daisy, an understated and slightly mad woman. Mia felt that the script treated her character too vaguely. After the film opened Mia said, "Daisy was harder to play than you would think. Perhaps I was trying to be something that I wasn't."

One part the role called for was for Mia to be in love with Robert Redford, and great controversy developed over how the two stars really did feel about each other. Mia said of Redford, "Robert was an interesting example of a man who looks like a perfect superstar, but underneath it all was, and liked being, extremely ordinary. Frankly I think he's intimidated by famous actors and the way he kept mentioning Barbra Streisand, one could tell he was starstruck."

Mia was incensed when the British newspaper the *Sun* carried a story that suggested she didn't care for Redford at all. Entitled "How Do You Kiss a Man That You Can't Stand?" the article quoted Mia as saying, "Every time a love scene came up I had to bite my tongue." Before Mia had an opportunity to deny the remarks, *Newsweek* ran an item about them, including the additional line supposedly from Mia that said, "Redford thinks he's the greatest actor in the world, that he knows everything and anyone else is inferior, especially women." Angry at the *Sun*'s suggestion and at *Newsweek*'s reprinting of it, Mia sued the *Sun* for libel in an English court and won an award for over $5,000.

While things were not as chilly between them as the press had reported, Redford did have greater trouble working on the film than Mia. He was uncomfortable with the fine microscope that Paramount had turned on the picture. Redford had no interest in Paramount's hype ideas and categorically refused to pose for a series of Robert Bruce clothing ads. "Drape me up like a *Vogue* model?" he said. "No way."

In recalling his own experience on the project Redford said, "We just prayed we could get finished with our work before the tent crumpled in on us or was simply blown away. The storm, of course, was all that hype and promotional bullshit Paramount arranged that threatened to destroy us all."

The actor had difficulty with Gatsby's manner of speaking and complained that the lines in the script did not allow Gatsby to speak like a real person. Redford knew that he and Mia would face the brunt of the criticism if the movie were a critical failure. *Time* magazine set the stage for the movie's difficulties in an article before its release that said *Gatsby* is "like the celebrity who was always called 'famous.' Famous for what? Famous for being famous."

In the eyes of the critics the movie was a famous failure. One wrote of Mia, "She comes, she goes, but in the end she just fades away."

Paramount executive Frank Yablans was so stung by the critical reaction that he gave a public speech to the National Television Academy in New York City. He said, "Never before has a film been so brutalized because it was so oversold. No picture has received more universal disdain. Even my kids asked me why we made it.

"We never said *Gatsby* was a great picture. All we said was, 'after seeing *Gatsby*, go out and buy some pots and some pans, or scotch, or get a haircut.' We believe the general public will respond to the film no matter what the critics say. After all, the average theatergoer is not a lobotomy victim."

The Great Gatsby turned out to be profitable, but it was not the great moneymaker the executives anticipated. Mia's brief return to stardom, not the resounding success she had hoped for, encouraged her to return to England and her family and continue with stage work. Mia's career would falter somewhat as she had more important things to attend to. Mia would engage in a winning battle against the United States Congress to adopt more children, and in a losing battle to save her marriage to Previn.

CHAPTER 8

MAMA MIA

*P*REGNANT, Mia left the set of *The Great Gatsby* and returned home to André Previn and their children. As all of Mia's friends and loved ones had discovered when she gave birth to Previn's twins four years earlier, the role of mother was the most important one in Mia's life.

In 1970, when Mia was twenty-four and pregnant, it was clear that her life was taking on a new dimension. Recalled one friend, "Some actresses are waiting for that big break, that one part that will make them a star. Not Mia. Ever since she was married to Sinatra, the only thing she was waiting for was to be a mother. She has wanted to have children for such a long time. Children mean everything to her."

Mia was thrilled and satisfied with the experience of

being a parent, and the twins were only the beginning. Mia spoke of the meaning of motherhood. "I like acting," Mia said, "but children come first. Some people make work their personal lives, but I chose to have a family. That's my career.

"I am from a large family and it seems to me that the benefits are enormous. My brothers and sisters are still my best friends and I want to re-create that environment.

"After I gave birth to my sons, I decided to adopt overseas because there are so many orphans who need families."

With the long war in Vietnam coming to end, Mia was deeply touched by the widespread reports of the tens of thousands of orphans left in the wake of battle. Mia became closely involved with an organization, Friends of Children (now defunct), that was active in the early 1970s helping people with adoptions. Mia, who had retained her American citizenship even though she and Previn lived mostly in Surrey, England, felt it was important that each of her adopted children also be given American citizenship.

Mia and Previn adopted two Vietnamese girls, Lark Song and Summer Song. Perhaps in admiration of her mother's noted film role, Summer Song later changed her name to Daisy. Mia felt that the two girls made excellent playmates and companions for her twin boys.

While they were very young, the four children almost lost their mother. One day when Previn was away and Mia and all the children were alone at their rural country home, Mia's appendix ruptured. As she telephoned for help, her panicked kids were too young to do anything for her. An ambulance raced to Mia's home, and as they were preparing to transport her, Mia insisted that one of the drivers remain with her children until a neighbor could come and look after them. "The thought of her leaving her children on their own upset her so much that she just stuck it out, desperately hoping the stomach pains would go away. She wouldn't leave until one of the drivers promised he would stay with the children," recounted Maureen O'Sullivan. Mia was rushed to King's College Hospital in London for an emergency appendectomy. The surgery was unexpectedly difficult, and complications set in. "For three days, it was touch and go whether she'd make it," said a hospital nurse. "Even in her moments of semiconsciousness, when she was struggling for her life, the only words we managed to understand from her were the names of her children." Two additional operations in quick succession were required to save Mia.

Mia was able to return to her home in just a few days to began a process of recovery that took several weeks. Mia's mother Maureen came to help look after the children, and Previn returned from one of his tours.

Shortly after Mia returned home, word spread through the British press of the near-fatal experience, and rumors began to fly that Mia had attempted suicide in response to Previn's purported infidelities. Said one close friend, "The reports of suicide were total rubbish, typical of the British press looking for any new angle to exploit. The last thing in the world Mia would ever do is to bring harm to herself. She loves her children much too much for that nonsense. Besides, Mia believes that suicide is a sin. The basis of the reports was Previn's dallying around. Now that may have driven some other women over the brink, but not Mia."

Once fully recovered, Mia again began the delicate juggling act of being a mother to four children and still spending time on her career. At the same time new public reports appeared about André Previn's own version of juggling. In 1975, British press reports quoted Previn, who would often leave his wife and children to tour as head conductor with the London Symphony Orchestra, as "hating to come back to an empty hotel room."

Previn was romantically linked with two women, Gillian Widdicombe and a stewardess for British Airways. Mia and Previn were to remain married for three more years, but it was clear that the marriage no longer included an exclusive romantic commitment to each other.

Said a friend, "By the time Mia had her twins, and her two girls, she was so blissfully happy being a mother that she really looked the other way when André would do his dabbling. She would look the other way until it became so painfully obvious that his affairs were reported in the papers. Then Mia became very upset."

With her marriage in a troubled state, Mia accepted a role in a new television production of *Peter Pan*. Mia was convinced that her children would love seeing her play the part as much as she enjoyed doing it. The *Hallmark Hall of Fame* production featured Mia as Peter Pan and Danny Kaye in the dual roles of Mr. Darling and Captain Hook. Mia was pleased to have the opportunity to sing professionally, and she loved the special effects involved with the production. Mia said, "When I was finished with the role I felt I could fly without wires."

Mia wasn't the only one fooled by the special effects. Although Mia often brought her four children with her on the set, where they would see their mother attached to special wires for the flying sequences, when the program was actually televised, the children actually thought that she could fly. After the program aired, Lark Song, who was just a toddler, shouted to Mia, "Please, Mother, please fly around the room." Mia declined, telling her daughter, "Not tonight, dear; it has to be a special occasion."

Mia was so happy in her role as a mother that she was horrified to learn of the high rate of abortions taking place in both the United States and England. In February 1976 Mia presented a voluminous antiabortion petition at the House of Commons on behalf of the Society for the Protection of Unborn Children, a conservative "prolife" organization in England that was against abortion. Mia was a staunch supporter of the antiabortion cause. "This is a matter of life and death," she declared. "I started getting involved in this issue after the birth of my twins; it made me realize just how important life is." Later that year, with her marriage to Previn once again at a calm point, and *Gatsby* finished, Mia gave birth to her third son, Fletcher.

Mia simply loved the infant boy, whose birth convinced her that she wanted even more children, and as she had done after the birth of her twins, she again wanted to adopt. But this time there was the threat of legal problems. When Mia had adopted Lark Song and Summer Song, she was able to have American citizenship granted to her two daughters, but now that she wanted to adopt again she encountered an American law which simply said that she couldn't.

In May 1977, amidst varying reports on the status of her marriage with Previn, Mia decided to adopt another child, this time from Korea. The youngster's name was Soon-Yi, and she had spent the majority of her six years in an orphanage in Seoul. Mia was eager to arrange for the adoption and was stunned to discover that federal law limits any one American family from adopting more than two foreign children.

Recalled another adoptive parent friend of Mia's, "Most people would have been daunted by the prospect of trying to get around the clear-cut federal law forbidding more than two foreign adopted children per family. But not Mia. Her instincts to be a mother brought out the fighter in her. Mia knew that she was going to adopt Soon-Yi and she was going to do it in accordance with the law. If that meant that the law was going to have to be changed so be it.''

Mia set out to change the federal law. But before she engaged in her major battle to do that, she first wanted to make certain that she would be with Soon-Yi, no matter what. To that end Mia was able to get the Justice Department to grant "parole status" to Soon-Yi, which allowed Mia to bring the little girl into the United States.

Once mother and daughter were granted the right to be together, Mia was determined to get the law changed so that Soon-Yi could become legally hers. In order to do that Mia had to find a congressional representative to sponsor legislation to change this long-standing federal law. Based on pressure from Mia, Representative Michael Harrington from Massachusetts sponsored the special bill, repealing the old law. Congress passed the bill, and Mia was free to adopt Soon-Yi.

With the battle behind her, Mia flew to Seoul to help arrange and supervise the transport of Soon-Yi and dozens of other children from the orphanage there to the United States. Mia recalls, " 'Once the Justice Department granted Soon-Yi the right to come to the United States, I just knew that I could get the entire law changed. There are many people like me who thrive on children, who love them so, and the need for adoptive parents is so great worldwide, that the law had to be changed. I'm pleased it was. But I am mostly pleased for me, because I have my beautiful Soon-Yi with me.''

Cheryl Markson, executive director of Friends of Children of Various Nations, a licensed international adoption

agency, said that Mia was an important force in helping
to get the law changed: "It used to be that adoptive families
were limited to two visas, which are called 9600 visas, for
bringing a child into the U.S. for the purpose of adoption.
It was a groundless restriction since every family has to be
approved for each and every adoption on its own merits.

"Changing the law has had an important impact on
many families, those who wanted to adopt more than two
children, like Mia, or in some cases families who've experienced those tragic problems in adopting a child from
Southeast Asia."

Mia's incredible drive that caused Congress to change a
law came as no surprise to those who knew her during her
marriage to André Previn. Mia was a mother first, and her
instincts to be a mother and an actress were foremost in
her life. Mia had spent time earlier as a quiet English country housewife, but those days were now over. Mia again
was enlarging and changing her life. It became more and
more clear, through what appeared to be a mutual choice,
that André Previn was becoming a less and less important
part of Mia's life.

Some two years after the first reports of his infidelity
were made public, it was clear that, romantically, Mia and
Previn were leading virtually separate lives. Mia was anxious to move all her children back with her to the United
States. A friend recalled, "Mia knew that she had more
than enough love to give her children for any two parents.
She didn't think it was healthy for her six children to be
in an environment where it was clear that the mother and
father didn't feel close to each other anymore. She wanted
to put some distance between herself and André."

During this time Mia made a series of films in which
she costarred with many other actors. Among these pic-

tures were *A Wedding, Death on the Nile, Avalanche,* and *Hurricane.* Mia, a well-known actress at this point in her career, could command up to a quarter of a million dollars for a single screen appearance. Sensing the dissolution of her marriage, Mia said of these film roles, "I took things as they came because I had to. I have all these children to support. Living in England obviously limited my choices of films that came along. My career was on the back burner."

Mia braved a record summer heat wave to travel to Chicago to film director Robert Altman's *A Wedding.* Recalls Mia, "It was much more than hot and humid; it was the hottest summer in the Midwest ever." But Mia enjoyed her work with Altman, an unconventional director who is also known for the films *M★A★S★H* and *Nashville.*

"Working with Altman was a marvelous group experience that was exhilarating," she said. "He encourages you to take risks, to improvise, to make a real fool of yourself if necessary, and then makes a party out of seeing the 'rushes' later with all the actors present." While Mia was pleased with her professional experience, the results were disappointing. The film, which also starred actress Lillian Gish, was never widely released, and the few critics who did see the picture had little that was flattering to say about it.

Mia quickly went from Chicago to Cairo, Egypt, to work on the film *Death on the Nile,* based on the Agatha Christie mystery. Among Mia's costars on this project were Peter Ustinov, David Niven, and Bette Davis. Against the advice of doctors Mia brought two of her children, Fletcher and Soon-Yi, to Egypt with her.

"I was warned against taking any of the children to Egypt because of the heat, the change in diet, the injections for travel and all," she said. "But I wish I had taken all of the children with me, not just the two who I thought needed to be with me the most at this particular time."

Mia's remark was a reflection upon on how terribly difficult she felt it was to be separated for any length of time from any of her children. She said, "I have to be with my children every so often or I become miserable. It's better not to talk about them unless they're with me or I fall into tears."

But Mia was probably lucky just to have two of her children with her when in Egypt, as she endured very harsh conditions while filming. Mia recalled the filming when she said, "If the cast had been anything less than first rate, I don't know how we would have survived the weather. It was terribly hot and there were a few sandstorms."

Much of the film took place on a luxury yacht cruising the Nile, and Mia and the other cast members watched in horror as several members of the crew fell overboard during the filming of particular scenes. They were rescued, but Mia was not so fortunate in avoiding other difficulties associated with the area. Despite treating her drinking water, Mia became very ill. She said, "I can tell that Nefertiti's revenge is every bit as lethal as Montezuma's."

In addition to internal bugs, Mia and the rest of the production company battled with huge flies and other creatures. Mia said, "Anytime we got the smallest morsel of food, the flies began gathering, so we learned to always eat indoors." During one meal stop in a posh Egyptian hotel, Fletcher and Soon-Yi heard their mother scream as Mia discovered a living spider in a plate of spaghetti she was eating.

The greatest hardship to one as sensitive as Mia was witnessing the terrible poverty of the area. Mia was deeply affected by all that she saw. She recalled, "In Aswan we saw little children carrying their infant siblings through the streets and although the little ones' faces were often covered with flies, their big brothers or sisters didn't even try to swat them off. By then I had gotten sick a few times, from sheer revulsion."

Mia returned to England after the film, and by this point the marriage with Previn was virtually over. A friend recalled, "Mia had some hopes that maybe doing all these movies would again pique André's interest in her, and her interest in him. It didn't. André had other girlfriends, and Mia was about to have some romantic entanglements of her own."

Leaving all her children in their father's care, Mia left England for Bora Bora to costar in the disaster film *Hurricane*. Mia was again given a large salary to costar with Jason Robards, Max Von Sydow, Trevor Howard, and Timothy Bottoms. Mia accepted the part primarily for financial reasons, and she chose to leave her youngsters behind because of the extraordinarily harsh climate in Bora Bora and because of the deadly insects there.

Hurricane was a disaster film both for its plot and because the entire production turned out to be one of the most difficult and unpleasant professional experiences Mia ever had. During filming, she explained why she had left the kids at home. "The place is lovely in itself but the weather and the bugs are calamitous. The tension on the set is high, the language isn't fit for a child's ears and I'm just hoping it's all over before too long."

The considerable tension on the set was caused by the weather, which was excessively hot and humid, and by the actions of producer Dino de Laurentiis. De Laurentiis had built a luxury hotel in Bora Bora to accommodate the cast and crew of the film, but the hotel was incomplete by the time filming took place, and it was an uninviting place to stay. To add insult to injury, de Laurentiis insisted on charging the cast and crew the full tourist rate to stay in the hotel, thus cutting deeply into the generous living allowance that each cast member was given. One said, "It looked like a great deal. We were given all this money to live on, and then we had to live there, and it was awful, and cost all the money we had been given."

But there was more than just money trouble for Mia on the set of *Hurricane*. She and costar Timothy Bottoms had a fierce free-for-all fight on the set, which resulted in Mia's getting a nasty gash on the chin that required sixteen stitches. Said a cast member, "The fight was a huge blow-up over nothing. Timothy didn't want to be there, Mia wanted to go home to be with her kids, everybody was unhappy. At one point Timothy made some sort of off-color remark to Mia, and she just slugged him, and he punched her right back. They just went at it for a while. They were fighting both each other and the situation they both were in. It took a couple of members of the crew to pry them apart from each other."

Mia, faced with the bad situation in Bora Bora and knowing that when she returned to England she was going to have to deal with the dissolution of her marriage to Previn, had finally allowed all her pent-up emotions to explode. But the fight with Bottoms wasn't the end of Mia's physical battles.

Shortly thereafter, Mia was injured during the filming of the climactic hurricane sequence. She was placed in a lifeboat, operated by a hydraulic lift, that was to rock wildly during the film. The lift malfunctioned and violently threw Mia against the side of the boat, bruising her badly and requiring a trip to the hospital. Said the cast member, "This scene was supposed to show the violence and the force of the hurricane, and in their quest for realism, the technicians had set this boat to rock like mad. But no one told Mia just how violent the thrusts were going to be, and the moment the boat started moving, Mia was tossed around like a rag doll. The boat was stopped after a few moments, but Mia was really tossed around, and really hurt."

Hoping to ease the pain of that injury, and the emotional scars she was carrying with her, Mia sought comfort in the arms of the noted Swedish cinematographer Sven Nykvist. Nykvist has never confirmed that an actual romance took place, but word of their relationship spread so fast on the set that it wasn't long before newspaper reports picked up on it. In October 1978, the *New York Post* ran this item: "Don't mention Bora Bora to André Previn. That's where his wife Mia Farrow reportedly flipped for cinematographer Sven Nykvist, and is accordingly ready to flee the Previn home. Mia's been there for months making *Hurricane* along with Sven and it's said (as always) to be true love."

In England, the reports went further to suggest that Mia had become pregnant by Nykvist. These reports were so widespread that a spokesman for Mia had to publicly deny them, and insist that she wasn't pregnant because she was already considering what new film offers to do after *Hurricane*. The denials were correct, for Mia did not become pregnant by Nykvist.

By this time, Previn himself had found yet another new love, an English beauty named Heather Jayston, and after returning to England from the filming of *Hurricane*, Mia quickly decided it was time to officially end the marriage that had been over in the heart for quite some time. Again, as she did with Sinatra, Mia decided to handle the final details herself, and she flew to the Dominican Republic to get the divorce decree. Mia was through with her husband, but she had made an even deeper commitment to mother-hood than ever before.

Despite her two failed marriages, Mia remained a strong believer in the institution. When actress Kimberly Beck, whom Mia had worked with in *Peyton Place* over a dozen years earlier, invited Mia to her wedding, she recalls a touching message Mia sent to her.

"When we worked together on *Peyton Place*," Beck said, "Mia used to always tell me that I was magic. When I got married and invited her to the wedding, she was busy filming *Hurricane* and couldn't come to California for the ceremony. But while she was on the *Hurricane* set she made the most beautiful thing for me.

"It was a very sweet letter which was framed in velvet and lace. She had placed little decals of angels around the border. At the end of the letter she wrote: 'Don't forget you're magic.' It was just such a lovely and supportive thing to do for me. You could tell that she had taken a lot of time, and put a great deal of care and thought into what she had written and how she had made it. It more than made up for her not being able to attend the actual cere-mony. Mia was there for me with her wonderful wishes and her beautiful spirit."

With her own marriage over, Mia was now busily get-ting her and her children's lives in order. The first step for Mia was to move from England back to America. Mia gathered all the children, except for Matthew and Sascha, who were in boarding school, and came to New York.

Mia and the children first settled at Maureen O'Sullivan's Central Park West apartment. Mia's mother's home would become the children's main residence. But before finally settling in New York, Mia wanted to make up for the time she had been separated from her children, and spent nearly a year with them in the privacy and comfort of a country home she had acquired on Martha's Vineyard.

Mia did not make a movie in 1979 and didn't work at all until late that year. Instead she devoted herself solely to being "Mama Mia," a fitting epithet bestowed upon her by the press. Mia and the children loved their time at Martha's Vineyard. Said Mia, "I'm very good alone. Sometimes weeks would go by when I didn't speak to another adult. I don't like strangers in the house and without help, looking after six children does keep one busy.

"Cooking, playing house, being Mama, driving the Jeep to school on those long rutted roads. I listened to Bach and Mahler. And during this period I read *War and Peace* —it took me three months.

"It's a beautiful place and one never tires of walking and looking out and listening. I have a big gray house, strong against the weather.

"The whole experience with the children was so nice. I didn't work because I didn't have the urge. I can go long stretches when I'm just not interested in my career. Finally I did need the money and simply had to get back to work. A lovely play came my way."

The play, *Romantic Comedy*, was Mia's first time on the big boards of Broadway. For an actress who had established herself domestically in television and films, the return to the American stage was important and wonderfully successful. *Romantic Comedy* proved to be a great professional experience for Mia, a delightful comeback after the upset of *Hurricane.*

Mia was cast as Phoebe Cradock, a mousy fourth-grade English teacher who meets a noted playwright she has long idolized. The play spans the fourteen years of their relationship as they team up to write Broadway flops and hits. In the course of the play, Mia's Phoebe is transformed from schoolmarm to sophisticate.

Mia loved the play and working with her costar Anthony Perkins. The irony of their casting—the victim in *Rosemary's Baby* and the killer from *Psycho*—was not lost on critics. Perkins was called on to perform a nude scene in the play, and reacting to her naked costar became one of Mia's favorite scenes. "I'm the only one who hardly sees him, because I am looking away, portraying embarrassment," she said.

The play was a critical and financial success. Mia surprised the critics, who had predicted that her physical stature, still frail and waiflike, would prevent her from performing believably on the large proscenium. But Mia was able to speak loudly and clearly and suppressed any doubts with her first few lines.

Mia also gave the play good notices. She told writer Cliff Jahr, "For me, what's new about *Romantic Comedy* is hearing people laugh. I'm used to silence out there in the dark, and that's if you're lucky. If the audience isn't out there coughing and shuffling. The laughter I have heard from the audience has actually moved me and changed my feelings.

"I'm awfully happy if the American theater people will have me. I mean, I love the long, instructive rehearsal period to get it right, the playing straight through without film's fragmentation. Making films is great fun, but I became bored with the roles I was being offered. How long can you play vulnerable, retiring women? Theater has been more rewarding in that respect because the material has been better."

During the play's tryout run, Mia brought four of the children with her to Boston. Jahr described what he saw there. "The sun-filled hotel room is filled with homey clutter: books, bent toys, squashed cookies, open jam jars, and unmade rollaway beds.

"Mia said, 'Yes, all this madness is absurd, but no more than the rest of my life. That would take Fellini to film. That is wonderful. I love it.' "

Most of all, Mia loves being a mother. After *Romantic Comedy* came to New York, she and the children moved into her mother's apartment again. With Maureen's blessing, Mia did some remodeling, knocking down a few walls and connecting the apartment with another unit to make it large enough for all the children.

Soon after her move to New York, Mia adopted another child. Mia's seventh youngster was handicapped. Little Moses, another Korean boy, has cerebral palsy. After Moses came to her home, Mia's oldest twins returned to her from England. Single parent Mia Farrow, at age thirty-four, was mother to seven live-in children. Her friend Richard Sylbert said, "Children are Mia's life. She's a walking advertisement for being a single parent. Mia is like an angel. She has more energy and caring than any ten women."

Maureen O'Sullivan, who also raised seven children, spoke of Mia's mothering to writer Kathy Henderson in *Redbook*. "Mia is very organized," said Maureen. "She has everything written down. What time the kids should be home, or why they aren't coming home.

"The twins are older so they can take charge of the younger ones, and they sometimes go to the studio when Mia is working. It all works out very well.

"Mia runs a very disciplined home. The children all have jobs to do—clean the kitchen floor, do the dishes, cook. You can go into the apartment at any time and it's very quiet. It's quite remarkable. Mia doesn't have any nannies. She has help that comes in, but Mia likes doing everything herself."

As Mia herself has said, "I was always able to take the children to work, and the older ones take care of the younger ones. I see them to school before I get to work, and I'm home by five or six in the evening.

"All I have done is cared about being a mother the way other actors have cared about their careers."

In speaking of motherhood, Mia expressed her deep satisfaction by saying, "It's paid off many times more than what I have done for them. I owe them so much more. I feel stronger now than in the past. As a mother of seven children I have to be strong.

"With me personal life comes first. Trying to understand children, to discover what fulfills them and makes them happy, fascinates me and gives me satisfaction. It brings something out of me which I probably need to give."

In 1980, Mia was firmly entrenched with her family in New York, deciding what her next career step would be. She was not actively pursuing a social life, merely pursuing her career part time while she concentrated on her full-time role as a mother. There was no way of knowing that a late dinner after her regular performance in *Romantic Comedy* would bring about a meeting with Woody Allen.

Or that Allen, normally a shy man, would be so enchanted with Mia that he would call her up and ask her out the very next day. Mia's life was about to go through yet another totally and unexpected change, this time involving America's most beloved comic genius.

CHAPTER 9

WORKING WITH WOODY

$\mathcal{M}$IA first met Woody Allen at a party in California many years before their fateful 1980 meeting. The initial meeting wasn't memorable for either: Woody was involved with Diane Keaton at the time, and the then-married Mia didn't have a wandering eye either. Mia says, "We first met at a party in California that Roman Polanski took me to. It was nothing more than a polite introduction."

The second meeting, at the popular New York City restaurant Elaine's, involved more than an introduction. Mia recalls, "Woody and I met again at Elaine's. After seeing me in *Romantic Comedy*, Michael Caine and his wife offered to take me to dinner. Woody was there, and we all talked. It was very nice."

Allen thought so too, for the very next day he phoned
Mia at her home and asked if she would like to have lunch.
Mia didn't hesitate, and the date was set. Said Mia,
"Woody asked me out to lunch, and we went to the Lutece
restaurant, we talked a lot and have been seeing each other
ever since."

Just a few months after their first date, it was clear that
Mia and Woody had become seriously involved in a com-
mitted and exclusive romantic relationship that continues
to this day. A friend of Mia's from New York City says,
"Mia is very faithful to the man that she loves. It just so
happens that the men in the two other major relationships
in her life drove Mia away. But Woody is just thrilled with
Mia and the feeling is mutual. They give each other just
what they each need. It is truly a remarkable relationship,
and as they have demonstrated over the last eight years,
they are both in this for the long haul."

Mia and Woody have merged more than just their hearts.
A few months after they first became involved they started
to work together; it has been a historic and successful collaboration between an actress and a screenwriter/director.
Mia and Woody have teamed up on more than half a dozen
movies, and it's likely that many more are planned. The
first project they did together was *A Midsummer Night's
Sex Comedy*, in which Mia played the ethereal Ariel, the
object of the amusing inventor Andrew's desire. Mia was
very concerned about her first professional undertaking
with Woody. She told Hollywood writer Barbara Lov-
enhein, "I was afraid that I would disappoint someone who
was a friend and whom I cared about. I kept saying, 'Are
you sure that you want me? Do you want somebody else?'
I was afraid I wouldn't be good enough and inevitably he
would be disappointed."

Sometime later, despite her success working with Woody, Mia told film critic Roger Ebert, "I always worry I won't be any good—you know. I'll fail completely and everyone will find me out. If I pull something off, I'm grateful and relieved."

Though Mia has never been entirely able to dismiss her self-doubts, Allen has never had any question about Mia's professional ability. In one of his rare interviews, he told entertainment writer Georgia A. Brown about his belief in Mia's talents. "She's an actress," he said. "She can play all sorts of characters. She has craft. She'll be modest about it, she'll be insecure about it, but when it comes down to it, she does it.

"She goes home, she learns her lines, she assumes accents, physical traits, every aspect of the character. And once you know she can do this, it opens up any number of possibilities."

Woody has taken great advantage of Mia's diverse acting abilities, forming for her characters as varied as Cecilia, the bittersweet waitress and dreamer from *The Purple Rose of Cairo*, and Tina, the sassy and streetwise aspiring actress in *Broadway Danny Rose*. The ability of this unique off-screen romantic collaboration to produce such varied on-screen characters is not lost on Woody.

"When I know a person intimately, I can write nuances and subtleties into a character that I want her to play," he says. "Originally I asked Mia to work with me because we were going out and I thought it would be fun. I've discovered through our working together that she's easy to work with because she is so competent. She's a professional who goes home and learns her lines. And she has a great sense of believability. You can give her anything to do and she will make it real."

Woody obviously enjoys working with Mia. With his characteristic understatement, he says, "I can do a lot more with her than I could do for a stranger."

Woody, who reveals little of himself in interviews, loves to talk about the talents of Mia. He told *New York Times* writer Michiko Kakutani, "Mia is capable of very, very, varied and interesting things, but like many actresses she never had a chance to do many of these things.

"She's always thought of as delicate and fragile, a sweet little thing. And sure, she can do that, and if you meet her that's what comes across. She has the ability to play a wide variety of things.

"I think it's good to write for someone. In trying to create a particular scene for a particular actress, it stretches them and it also stretches me.

"It's more fun to work this way with Mia because it has an exploratory quality to it—you don't get sort of stale doing the same thing. You either get a catastrophe or you get a very interesting project.

"I feel like I've lucked out working with Diane Keaton and Mia. I'm lucky that they've made this contribution to me. My contribution is relatively minimal. I can only provide the script and then they bail me out, they make me look good. People who say to Mia, 'Oh you're so lucky to be making films with him' don't realize the true situation.

"I am the one who's lucky to be able to work with someone who can do things consistently, who's stable, pleasant to work with with, who can execute my ideas, who's available to shoot my style, to reshoot too. I can just call up Mia and say, 'Let's go back and reshoot.' When you've got someone who has six other pictures to do, you can't have that luxury."

A Midsummer Night's Sex Comedy was obviously a rewarding experience for both director and star, so much so
that they have continued the winning partnership. Since
1981, Mia has starred in every film Woody has made. The
close personal and working relationship is reminiscent of
Woody's filmmaking idol Ingmar Bergman and his long
romantic and professional association with actress Liv Ull-
mann.

After *Sex Comedy*, Mia played the psychiatrist trying to
cure the madcap character of *Zelig*. In Woody's most technically daring film to date, Mia was cast as Dr. Eudora
Fletcher, the only person in the world who tried to help
Zelig, the tragicomic "chameleon man."

From there Mia and Woody went on to one of Allen's
most pure all-out comedies, the wild *Broadway Danny Rose*.
In *Danny Rose* Mia took her biggest departure from playing
the perennial undernourished waif. Instead she was the
tough, street-smart "Broadway babe" Tina Vitale.

The role, which required a Brooklyn accent and body
padding to completely transform Mia into Tina, was
among Mia's most challenging. Mia said, "Tina was too
different for me and I was scared, until I shot the first day.
Then I realized I could do it."

Entertainment writer Michiko Kakutani described the
character of Tina: "No doubt you've seen a woman who
looks like her . . . maybe sipping daiquiris at the time in
Caesar's Palace or chain-smoking in some chintzy nightclub in New York. She wears ruffled shirts, tight slacks
and a gold name chain around her neck. She keeps her
blond hair in a 1950s 'do,' and never goes anywhere, even
at night, without a pair of sunglasses clamped firmly on
her nose."

Mia said that when she finished the script, "I didn't know

if I could do it. I sort of have doubts about everything that I do and maybe with this there was more than the usual fear. Tina was such a different character and I wasn't sure how I would get there or anything."

The genesis of the Tina character struck Mia and Woody years before *Broadway Danny Rose* was made. The two were sitting at an Italian restaurant when they caught sight of a gum-chewing, chain-smoking woman wearing sunglasses, whose blond bouffant hairstyle stood six inches straight up. Woody made strict mental notes of her mannerisms, and when he needed a comic foil for his failing agent Danny Rose, the image resurfaced.

Mia spoke to film critic Gene Siskel about the research and effort that went into preparing Tina's voice. "I realized," she said, "that it was essential to toughen up my own voice and that's what came out. And I tried to find a Brooklynese accent. Using my own natural voice would have submerged my whole effort.

"So I taped some people like that because I wanted the accent to be consistent. There was this secretary at Orion Pictures [Allen's production and distribution company] who talked like that. I invited her and a couple of her friends to come over and they sat in my kitchen and chatted about a whole bunch of things. I taped it and I played it over and over.

"And I had a tape of *Raging Bull* [the film staring Robert DeNiro], and they all spoke like that in the movie. So I played that a few times. Lowering my voice was just a matter of mental adjustment."

The transformation of Mia into Tina was visual as well as vocal: bingeing on pasta and other foods, Mia added over a dozen pounds to her small frame. She also wore large foam pads, to give Tina a more curvaceous figure.

Mia. had lengthly conversations with Woody about the substantive aspects of the role. She recalls, "We didn't sit down and have whole discussions about acting. But because Woody knows me well and I know him, he knew the key things to say, and it saved a lot of time.

"Woody knows what I can and can't do better than myself. Woody has changed my view of my work, by just assuming I could do all these things."

Woody gives the credit for the successful creation of Tina to Mia: "Mia mentioned it would be fun playing that kind of woman, just to try it, and I took her seriously. I think she somehow, down deep, felt, maybe without knowing it herself, that she could do that kind of thing.

"I have always wanted to do something about that whole milieu and when she mentioned that, one thing led to another in my mind over a period of time and it sort of fell into place."

Broadway Danny Rose was the third film Mia and Woody made together, and Mia appreciated the fact that Woody went out of his way to hire many of the same crew who had worked on the previous films. Despite her extensive film experience, Mia has never enjoyed working with totally different people from one project to the next. Working on a brand-new set "was scary. It was that feeling that it was just some accident that they ended up using me instead of someone else and with every movie I felt like I had to prove myself all over again. I think I did somewhat better with longer parts because each week that you work with the same people, you feel a little safer and therefore a little more productive."

With Woody, Mia was able to enjoy feeling secure on the set. A not-nervous Mia was a better actress, and she knew it. "With *Midsummer Night's Sex Comedy*, I felt like a rank amateur. With *Zelig*, I felt I was getting friendlier with everyone. And now, after *Danny Rose*, working is the best it's ever been for me."

But, as always, Mia was quick to qualify her own positive feelings, by adding, "It can all disappear in a minute. I have more confidence than I have ever had before. I think that when you're working with people and you feel that they're not judging you, it makes you feel a little freer to just try stuff.

"Woody writes so beautifully, so to start with the scripts are good. And Woody knows what ought to be done. By extension, I feel surer of what I'm doing. With the characters I have played before, it was just a shot in the dark —you had to go on your hunches and some were wrong. Some were right."

Mia's positive experiences on Woody's films enabled her to realize that some of the professional missteps in her past were not entirely her fault. "When I played Daisy in *The Great Gatsby*, I found the role difficult and elusive. I kept losing her because the director's vision was not clear, and neither was mine. But Woody doesn't allow that. He keeps you on a steady course and doesn't let you wander away from his view of things."

Those close to Mia agree that aside from the support and satisfaction of the personal relationship with Woody, as an actress Mia is in an ideal position to be guided and encouraged by a man who loves her to do her very best work.

Richard Sylbert, the highly respected film production designer who has known Mia since working with her in *Rosemary's Baby*, notes that Mia is in a position for which many other actresses would sacrifice their eyeteeth. "For someone who wants a career," says Sylbert, "and who wants to act, and who wants to do all the other things that Mia does, she is in the best possible position. She's with Woody. A huge portion of his creative energy has gone into designing characters specifically for her.

"How many actresses can say that they have one of the world's truly great filmmakers writing with them in mind? Very few. How many actresses then go on to work with the same great filmmaker on a regular basis in a wide variety of roles? Fewer still. Mia is in a unique and wonderful situation. She's having her cake and being able to eat it too. Don't think for a minute there are not a lot of actresses who would love to be where Mia is right now. They are probably endless numbers of them."

Maureen O'Sullivan is thrilled for her daughter. Maureen sees Mia's collaboration with Woody as a perfect fit: she's in a stimulating creative environment and is enjoying the satisfying personal life O'Sullivan long sought for herself. She has said, "What Mia has with Woody is tremendously exciting for an actress. It's like a repertory company. The variety of parts Mia has been able to play, from Dr. Fletcher to the 'dese-dems-dose' dame in *Danny Rose*, is perfect for her way of acting.

"Mia thinks along the lines of a character actress. For example, she doesn't care how she looks; she wants to get the character right. Sometimes I would say, 'Lord, you aren't wearing your hair that way, are you? or 'You're going to wear glasses?' and she would say, 'Oh, yes, I need to be very plain in this part.' You understand Mia could out-glamourize anybody if she wanted to. If the part came along where she should be glamorous, then she would.

"Mia thinks as a character actress, but what she definitely has is star quality, and Woody sees that. Most actors are one or the other, either the star or the character actor. But Mia is really both."

Mia was given the opportunity to demonstrate her versatility in her fourth film under Woody's direction, *The Purple Rose of Cairo*. In this atmospheric tale of a Depression-era waitress whose love for the movies enables her to actually meet film characters who jump from the screen into her life, Woody stayed behind the camera entirely. The brunt of the acting chores fell strictly on Mia, who carried the role of Cecilia the waitress beautifully, earning high praise from critics, Woody, and the her fellow cast members.

Actor Jeff Daniels played the part of film actor Tom, who stepped off the screen into Mia's life. Daniels, who has played opposite such current screen favorites as Debra Winger, thought working with Mia was wonderful. He told writer Georgia A. Brown, "Mia's approach is very simple, very straightforward. She doesn't junk it up. It's very difficult to stay simple. I know because I try and then I start stuttering, doing all these gestures so I look like a windup toy whose coil broke. But Mia can do it like it's the most natural thing in the world and it's not."

In one particularly touching scene in the film, Daniels' character is beaten up on a church altar, and a shocked Mia races to comfort him. She is so stunned by his condition that she begins to weep. Daniels was especially impressed with Mia's ability to cry on command.

"It looked like something out of *Rambo*," he says. "Mia comes over to me where I'm lying on the floor and she's got to say, 'Oh Tom, poor Tom, lay your head on my chest,' and then cry.

"Well, Mia just puts down her knitting, comes over, sits down and she does it. And then she does it again. She did it maybe ten times.

"Woody, after seven takes or so, would say, 'Can't we have a different lighting on that?' or 'Could you just cry on the line just after the one you cried on before?'

"And Mia could do it. Exactly as she was asked. I was really impressed. I couldn't do that. I was doing everything I could not to blow whatever line I had. But she nailed it every time.

"It wasn't like the usual, 'Could you give me a little more glycerin?' or whatever they put in your eyes to make you cry. Mia would just wait about five seconds and then start in and sure enough, there'd come the tears. Finally Woody says, 'Okay, I think we've got it,' and Mia would go back to her knitting."

Mia herself was pleased with the role in *Purple Rose*, and she acknowledged that many aspects of the character undoubtedly were the result of Woody's knowing her so well. "She's a nice character, very simple and ingenuous, and I liked her. I think she's a lot better than I am, but I can identify with some parts of her and she is closer to me than some of the other characters I have played. She is sweet and innocent and really a good person, who is trying very hard to cope with her lot in life."

Added Woody, "What I saw was merely that she could play this part. I wrote the movie because I liked the story and that was the part I conceived for her."

The role in *Purple Rose* again forced Mia to come up with another unique vocal characterization, but unlike her experience in *Broadway Danny Rose*, this time the voice she needed just came to her. She recalls the voice's incarnation: "It was my first day on the set, and that voice just came out. This character was the closest in a way to my own. It's either something I've played before or something that I was or I am. I didn't have to force any of the reactions or the feelings."

The character of Cecilia was obsessed with the movies. Mia identified with this obsession: "She has an absolute commitment to the movies. I too can be completely absorbed in the reality of a movie. I would visit sets often as a child, I can remember sitting in John Wayne's tall chair, but I never put that together with the finished product. I remember that I loved *Gone With the Wind* and *Lawrence of Arabia*, and everything that was on television."

Mia and Woody's fifth film together, *Hannah and Her Sisters*, provided a glimpse into the private Mia. Fans who were interested in her personal life couldn't have asked for a more vivid view of what Mia was really like than in *Hannah*. The majority of the movie was shot in Mia's Central Park apartment, and the film costarred her mother Maureen O'Sullivan. Woody himself described the picture as "a romanticized view of Mia."

Mia enjoyed working on this film, especially as it was her first professional work with her mother. But working with Maureen for the first time made Mia a bit nervous. "It was intimidating," she said. "We only had one scene together and in the middle of it I found myself thinking, 'My goodness, she's good!'

"It was nice too because Woody was admiring of her performance. He was just raving, which he hardly ever does, so I was real proud of her."

Woody was pleased not only with O'Sullivan's work but with the outcome of the entire picture. Still he acknowledged that while *Hannah* was not as technically difficult to film as *Zelig* or *The Purple Rose of Cairo*, the writing and directing of this "romanticized view of Mia" was anything but simple. He said, "This was the hardest thing we've done. There was so much ambivalence to the character, her goodness, her too-goodness, her niceness to her sisters, but her feeling superior to them. In order to be successful, the character had to move in and out of all those feelings throughout the picture."

Mia too recognized the difficulty of trying to play a part based somewhat on her own personal characteristics. "It was hard," she said. "Because it was subtle, not flamboyant like Tina from *Broadway Danny Rose* or like the other two sisters in this film. Their parts were clearly defined. In this case, we found the character as we went along, rather than having it from the start."

Shortly after *Hannah*, Woody chose to do a film based somewhat on his own life. In *Radio Days*, Mia joins a large ensemble cast to play a popular radio singer. This film, set in the 1940s, demonstrated Woody's great attention to period detail. The budget was high, his largest ever, and while there were never any out-and-out fights during the filming, Woody found making the film somewhat stressful. It was clear that Woody doesn't save all of his praise for Mia, or all of his criticism for others.

Mia's *Radio Days* costar Danny Aiello noted Woody and Mia's somewhat strained working relationship. He told writer Georgia A. Brown, "He can be very devastating. I think I saw her tear up once; maybe I'm wrong and it was for something else, but she's a very emotional young lady. They have an understanding. There is with Woody a slight intimidation factor. He's very precise in everything that he does, very tough but in a way that's not verbal, not emotional, very quiet. He will scold, but in this quiet way. His screen persona is meek, but he's not that way at all. And he's no different with Mia."

But despite slight rough spots caused by the budget pressures and difficulties of filming, *Radio Days* went on to success, and the working relationship and the romance between Woody and Mia was only strengthened.

Actor Wallace Shawn told Brown, "I feel Mia enjoys the fantasy of playing someone not herself and dressing up in a costume the way a child or an adolescent enjoys it. She acts with a certain light touch that young people have when they act, when they dress up and pretend. You can see the child enjoying it and I felt I was seeing this in her."

Mia and Woody's most recent collaboration is the dramatic film *September*. Woody, always the perfectionist, actually shot the film twice. During the first filming, Mia was again happily teamed with Maureen O'Sullivan. But Woody, not faulting any of the actors, was displeased with the results of the first *September*. While Mia retained her role, the majority of the remaining parts were reshuffled to members of the original cast or were totally recast. O'Sullivan was not in the second version. Critics applauded Woody's effort to again diversify into drama but faulted the movie for being overly bleak.

Given their many successes on the screen, there is no sign that Mia and Woody will not continue to work together far into the future. Mia has said, "I love working with him. It's terrific because he's so sure of himself and that's how it ought to be, what's right and what's true. It makes it so much easier to contribute because you know the thrust of where you should be going with something. He gives me confidence. I need a little extra anyway and just knowing I'm in his capable hands is so supportive."

Mia and Woody's on-screen efforts are there for the world to see. But their private lives would make for another series of wonderfully romantic films. After many romantic ups and downs, each has finally found the right partner, and they have sealed the partnership with the joint adoption of one child and the birth of another.

CHAPTER 10
THE PERFECT
PARTNERSHIP

$\mathcal{M}$IA remains part of an extended family. Her ties with her own children are close, and she remains just as close to her brothers and sisters and her mother as she did when she was growing up.

Maureen O'Sullivan remarried in 1983 and moved out of the apartment she had shared with Mia and the children. But Maureen has long remained in the public eye, working steadily in films and on television. In a postscript which shows that Mia's great kindness must be an inherited trait, Maureen had a tender bedside reunion with her *Tarzan* costar Johnny Weissmuller in 1980.

The actor, who had long been ill, was on his deathbed at the Motion Picture Home in Los Angeles. Weissmuller's family located Maureen and told her that it was one of

Johnny's last requests to see her again. The two had not
spoken for over twenty years.

Quickly Maureen left New York to travel to California.
Veteran entertainment reporter Tony Brenna greeted
O'Sullivan at the Los Angeles International Airport and
took her to Weismuller's bedside. Brenna recalls, "Johnny's health was failing; he was suffering from a protracted
respiratory ailment. He was frail and in bad shape. He was
in terrible spirits and had expressed to his family that he
wanted to see Maureen, his former *Tarzan* costar, as a
reminder of the good old days.

"Johnny's family felt that Maureen might be able to life
Johnny's sagging spirits. They called her in New York and
asked her to come for a visit.

"Maureen didn't even have to think twice. She was
genuinely concerned about Johnny's health and caught the
first plane she could to the coast. The reunion worked
wonders. The moment Maureen entered his hospital room
and approached his bedside, Johnny's face just lit up in
a huge smile. Maureen went right up to him and gave
him a big hug, took his hand and said, 'Me Jane, you
Tarzan.' They both laughed. Johnny was just beaming.
Maureen and Johnny spent hours together talking and
reminiscing.

"Maureen told me, 'You never give up on the people
you care about. When you're a friend, you're a friend for
life. That is a something I believe and that I have passed
on to all my children and grandchildren. I know that they
believe it too.'

"Maureen's care and love for a man she hadn't seen in
so many years was just amazing. It's clear where Mia gets
a lot of her goodness, straight from her mother."

Mia took another new step when she decided as a single parent to adopt her handicapped son Moses. Mia recalls that she didn't make the decision alone. "When I moved to New York, I decided to adopt a handicapped child. I talked it over with the other children and we decided that we could do it.

"Moses is doing great—he wears a leg brace and has some weakness in his right side, but all the other children help with his exercises and the older ones take turns doing his therapy. It's been wonderful for all of us as a family."

As Mia and Woody became closer, they decided in 1985 to adopt a child together. Little Dylan is the apple of her father's eye. Woody was so pleased with his experience with Dylan that he was excited when in May 1987 Mia became pregnant again, with his own child. Woody told Roger Ebert, "My feelings about the baby are very complicated. You know Mia and I adopted a baby, Dylan, before she got pregnant, and there is absolutely no difference in the love that I will feel for the new child and the love I feel for Dylan. In fact I love Dylan so much that I would be pleasantly surprised if I love the baby we are having together as much as the one we adopted.

"I've noticed in recent months that a lot of people I know are having babies. Women friends will say that the biological clock is ticking and I tell them not to bother to get pregnant—just adopt. When I first met Mia and she was telling me about all the children she had adopted, I said, 'Oh, what a nice gesture,' and she said, no, I had it all wrong; it's not what she had done for them, it was what they'd done for her. Now I know how she felt."

As word of Mia's pregnancy spread, Woody told the

Associated Press about his feelings and his future plans with Mia. "I was very surprised. We were both surprised. It was nothing that we were planning particularly. It was just a sudden surprise and we were both sort of happy about it.

"This was an accident and then once it occurred, Mia would never think of having an abortion. And I don't think that I would either.

"I think I'll be profoundly wise and generous, liberal, understanding. I'd be surprised if I'd be less than a perfect father. The thing hasn't really sunk into me. Right now, it's in the early stages. But I think at some point when I'm actually confronted with the issue—with offspring—then I think I'll be delighted. I feel pleasant about it. I think it will be a good experience. I think it will deepen me. I hope so. Either that or it will put me in a crazy house. We have no plans that I know about to alter our extremely comfortable and viable living situation. I probably see as much of Mia as any married person would."

Film historian Thierry de Navacelle, who observed Woody and Mia together on the set of the film *Radio Days*, noted Woody's relationship with the children. "He has a nice relationship with the kids," de Navacelle said. "They were frequently on the set, and Dylan would call him 'Daddy.' Sometimes Woody would direct while holding the child in his arms."

Celebrity photographer David McGough has a special perspective about Mia and Woody. Initially he had an adversarial relationship with the couple, frequently stalking them all over New York City in an effort to get photos of them and their children. But in taking a cue from what happened to her with André Previn many years ago,

Mia suggested that a formal photo session might make photographers less anxious to shoot "grab-shots" on the street.

In March 1981 McGough was invited by Woody's agent to do a private shoot of the pair. He said, "I was face-to-face with them for the first time. It took time to adjust; I am used to photographing them as they run away. As kind of a making-up gift, I gave them a copy of my favorite photography book, Robert Frank's *The Americans*, and it opened them up a little.

"They were a perfect couple—holding hands, constantly kissing. I could tell that Woody was still uncomfortable. They never raised their voices above a whisper. Me, I was in shock. He's never done this with any photographer. I think he's finally coming out of his shell. Mia is a very special celebrity—in a word she is unique.

"Motherhood is her priority. To say she's a great mom is an understatement. She's a very caring, loving person. Mia and Woody just want to be left alone. They want to live as normal a life as they can. They try to keep the paparazzi away, just so they can live the life that they want to. I have worked out a very good relationship with them now. Woody calls me whenever an event takes place that he wants photographed and released to the press.

"In January of 1988 I photographed Mia and Woody and their little baby Satchel. They're such perfect parents—to watch them, you can just see the love that pours out for the baby. Mia is more beautiful, more attractive than she's ever been. She just gets prettier all the time. She still looks like she's in her twenties, she defies aging. She gives her kids more love than a dozen women. Mia takes her kids to the park, picnics, concerts, museums, just about everywhere. Recently Mia took the kids to the Big Apple Circus in Lincoln Center. Woody is great with Mia's kids—all of them, not just Satchel and the one he adopted, Dylan.

"Her apartment is huge—it takes up the whole floor. It has eleven rooms, seven bedrooms. It has a beautiful view of the park. It's a great place to raise a family."

McGough says that Woody and Mia's own private dating habits have changed somewhat. "I have noticed a change in Mia and Woody's preference for restaurants. They used to go to Elaine's a lot but not so much any longer. Now they are going to finer restaurants lately. Fancier ones, like Lutece, where they had their first big date so many years ago."

Mia and Woody are enjoying the comfort and stability a long-term relationship with children can bring. While they still have no plans to marry, they remain warm and close and productive together. It is still the perfect partnership.

But for the most part the partners are content to spend time in her apartment with the whole family. The twins Matthew and Sascha are now teenagers, as are Lark Song, Daisy, Soon-Yi, and Fletcher, who is interested in becoming a lawyer. The younger set starts with ten-year-old Moses, who remains in good health, and then the toddler Dylan, and finally little Satchel.

Says her friend Richard Sylbert, "Mia is, very simply, an amazing woman. She's living the life she wants with the man she loves. Her children are a daily source of pure delight, and her long career continues to flourish."

Years ago Mia spoke of doing everything in a big way. Now, happy in New York City with her successful relationship with Woody, her successful career as a featured actress in all his projects, and her successful family, Mia enjoys an incredibly busy, exciting, and varied life. She has already lived several lifetimes in her first four decades, and it's impossible to know how many she has ahead of her.

CHAPTER *11*

THE FILMS OF MIA FARROW

*I*T is no accident that Mia Farrow has inextricably woven a family life together with an acting career. Perhaps spurred by her mother's pent-up desire to act, both in films and on the larger stage of life, Mia has pursued her craft and her personal growth with vigor. But Farrow's devotion to her work and to that personal quest, often flamboyant in its own way, has always been characterized by a generosity and a devotion to family, both her own and the creative ensembles with which she has worked. What seems to be Mia's ideal romantic, professional, and now familial relationship with Woody Allen is actually the end result of a long struggle to find a balance between her professional ambition and her devotion to her natural, adopted, and creative families. These dual qualities can be attributed to a family that emphasized both.

Unlike other actresses of her generation, such as Barbra Streisand, Goldie Hawn, Sally Field, or Allen's former paramour Diane Keaton, Farrow has never given a "star" performance, and precisely because of this she has never garnered an Oscar nomination or the level of public favor that these and other actresses have attained. On the other hand, Farrow, at forty-one, is freer to play a wide variety of roles than most actresses her age. Having shed her image as helpless victim and waif—and never having had a particularly wide following as such—Farrow now polishes her craft, playing on a rich variety of leading character roles without having to worry about upholding an image of being tough, spunky, brittle, wholesome, or batty.

Farrow's brand of personal experimentation and devotion to the ensemble can be traced throughout her work as an actress, which divides into five periods: her initial appearance on *Peyton Place* through her divorce from Frank Sinatra in 1967; stardom from 1968 to 1971; the years coinciding with her marriage to André Previn, during which she made films primarily in England and France and *The Great Gatsby* in the United States, followed by a hiatus from film acting, a concentration on her family, and appearances only on the London stage; a period of regrouping, which saw her return to ensemble film work and a Broadway appearance, ending with her separation from Previn; and, finally, the Woody Allen years, during which the couple's personal life dovetailed with their films, whose handmade quality rejuvenated both careers. Perhaps because of her growing up with Hollywood as second nature, Farrow has at each stage concerned herself not with star trappings but with her craft and her family, a concern that sustains her even in the weakest of vehicles.

Farrow's overnight success as the tragically beset Allison MacKenzie in *Peyton Place* (1964–66) was due in large part to the popularity of Grace Metalious' trashy runaway best-seller of the same name and of the film version, which starred Lana Turner and Diane Varsi as the original Allison, and in large part to her own talent.

Mia clearly stood apart from the rest of the cast. Whereas other actresses of the '60s like Julie Christie, Faye Duna-way, and Ann-Margret did not hit their stride until their mid-twenties or later, Farrow's precociousness and mature screen presence enabled her to step into young adult roles at an age when her contemporaries were cast in smaller, supporting roles.

As a result, Mia was being cast in serious, "adult" lead-ing roles by age twenty. After roles in two relatively minor films, John Guillermin's *Guns at Batasi* (1964) and the ill-fated *A Dandy in Aspic* (1968), directed by both Anthony Mann and actor Laurence Harvey, Farrow made her true debut as a screen actress in American expatriate director Joseph Losey's *Secret Ceremony*, released in 1968, the same year as the release of *Rosemary's Baby*.

Losey, blacklisted in Hollywood in the 1950s and exiled to England (he never returned to the United States), created an idiosyncratic, highly personal body of film work that dealt most often with the theme of role reversal and role-playing, and through this reversal access to forbidden areas of class and sexuality. In both *Sleeping Tiger* (1954) and *The Servant* (1963), for example, Dirk Bogarde, cast in the first as a sociopathic killer taken in by a psychiatrist and his wife as part of an experiment in criminal rehabilitation and in the second as a menacing, devious butler, methodically becomes the master of someone else's house. In Losey's masterpiece, *The Go-Between* (1971; Palme d'Or, Cannes), his most fruitful collaboration with playwright Harold Pinter, a small boy at his relatives' estate plays the role of messenger between his irresponsible cousin and her secret, working-class lover. All three of these films derive their considerable power from the unspoken taboos they touch.

Secret Ceremony is in a sense the thematic standard of Losey's films, for it is entirely about role-playing, and it touches on incest and the mother-daughter relationship. By all rights this should make it one of Losey's most interesting films, but it is experimental even for Losey, a darling of the '60s avant-garde, and suffers from a muddled script. Nevertheless, the film is remarkable for its use of three Hollywood stars—Farrow, Elizabeth Taylor, and Robert Mitchum—in a work that is neither glamorous nor particularly sparing in its examination of their characters.

The first—and the most fascinating—third of the film takes place virtually without dialogue. The setting is London, gray and silent. Farrow, catlike, dressed in black and wearing a long black wig, follows Elizabeth Taylor onto a bus, to the cemetery, and to Taylor's daughter's grave. When Taylor asks, "What do you want from me?" Farrow's only response is "Mummy. Mummy." Through a few words, photographs, and their physical interplay, the two women reveal that Leonora's (Taylor's) daughter has been drowned, while Centhi's (Farrow's) mother has recently died, leaving the waiflike Centhi alone in a large house with her mother's possessions. In that house, the two women act out their grief and reenact their pain in the secret ceremony of the film's title. Leonora tries on Centhi's mother's stole: Centhi prepares Leonora breakfast. Centhi fervently believes that Leonora is her mother—and perhaps she is. The women's interaction is a play of masks, roles, identities. They reenact a drowning as they bathe together. "Can I crawl into bed with you?" asks Centhi. "Please, Mummy, can I?" Each makes compromises in order to maintain their mutual fantasy—but the truth begins to come out. Leonora, who looks exactly like Centhi's mother, may be a prostitute, and it becomes apparent that Centhi has had a sexual relationship with her stepfather, Albert (Mitchum), who appears on the scene to break up the two women's fantasy idyll, since she was ten or eleven. In the film's most extraordinary scene, Centhi acts out, by herself, the memory of a sexual liaison in the kitchen with her stepfather, which ends with the disordered, half-mute baby-woman cowering beneath a coffee table.

This psychodrama sets us up for a volatile second half, but the explosion never quite materializes. Leonora ultimately takes the disturbed Centhi on a seaside vacation in the hope of recapturing their fantasy world, but Albert follows. "I always make her feel like a woman," argues Albert to Leonora. "You make her feel like a retarded zombie." As Leonora's ideal begins to crumble, Centhi becomes the target of Leonora's resentment toward her real, vanished daughter. In the end, Leonora rips up Centhi's stuffed animals, symbolically destroying both Centhi's troubled childhood, in which Centhi's mother acquiesced, and their therapeutic ceremony; there is some hope that this role-playing has helped both women to exorcise their demons.

Secret Ceremony rightfully placed Farrow in the first rank of young American screen actresses. Although later that same year *Rosemary's Baby* would clinch Farrow's position as a major "bankable" star, *Secret Ceremony* showed that Farrow was willing to go (and capable of going) far beyond Allison MacKenzie. The scene in which she re-creates the sex act with her stepfather stretched the limits for any commercial film of that era, and twenty years later it still seems daring. Farrow's and Taylor's work together is particularly good, even if the film falls far short of Losey's clearly high aims. Farrow had proved that she would be able to hold her own with world-class directors and actors.

In spite of the enormous success of *Rosemary's Baby*, it is an unlikely film to be considered a modern classic. Ira Levin's cunning thriller depended in large part on establishing the believability—indeed the banality—of a witches' coven existing in the Dakota apartments in uptown Manhattan. Director Roman Polanski used his first American film to prove himself a talented international director, and to create that believability visually to say something about the banality of evil. Polanksi, whose family fell victim to the Nazis in Poland, uses every facet of the film—the costumes, the decor, the lighting—to hide from Farrow's Rosemary the evil around her, while still foreshadowing it every step of the way. Polanski, with cinematographer William Fraker, production designer Richard Sylbert, and costume designer Anthea Sylbert, creates an environment of typically casual American lushness in which everything is just right but also just wrong. Perhaps it took Polanski, a foreigner, with his tragic background and his mania for detail, to see clearly the potential for evil in the apparent benignity of American TV commercials and easy access to detergent, fine foods, and art. Polanski's mastery is that he doesn't overdo it.

As played by Ruth Gordon and Sidney Blackmer, Minnie and Roman Castevet, the heads of the coven next door, are crass and tacky, but never overly so. John Cassavetes, as Rosemary's husband, Guy, whose Faustian bargain it is to plant the devil's seed in Rosemary in exchange for a fast-track career, is never used by Polanski to portray "evil": Cassavetes' Guy is simply lazy, willing to give in, at the core inherently weak.

Farrow's Rosemary, then, in Polanski's and Levin's context, is "innocent" in that she is oblivious enough to be used. Rosemary has, if unwittingly, bought into that easy American lushness and her role as isolated, stay-at-home wife and mother-to-be. It is her freshness and spontaneity, typified by her saying to Guy, as they picnic on the bare floor of their new apartment, "Let's make love," that signals to her—too late—that she should trust her friend Hutch (Maurice Evans), the only character who sees through the material veneer of the witches' coven. Written shortly after the appearance of Betty Friedan's *The Feminine Mystique*, Levin's story, along with his later *The Stepford Wives*, revealed itself to be a feminist horror tale, on top of which Polanski overlaid his experience with Nazism.

Farrow's challenge was to play this transition—from happy homemaker to terrified witness—whose resistance comes too late to prevent the evil from procreating. Farrow, with the help of her talented costars and crew, met the challenge with a remarkably self-effacing performance. She is particularly good when she begins to unconsciously rebel against the demands of Guy and the Castevets, as when she returns home, to Guy's dismay, with a boyish Sassoon haircut to replace her soft girlish do. Rosemary develops an independent, protofeminist consciousness before our eyes, but not in time to stave off the horror. It is perhaps no accident that while playing this role Farrow ended her relationship with the domineering Sinatra.

With *John and Mary* (1969), Mia and Dustin Hoffman hit full stride as the most sought-after serious young American film actors of the day, Farrow on the heels of *Rosemary's Baby*, Hoffman following *Midnight Cowboy*. Directed by Peter Yates (*Bullitt, The Dresser*) and adapted from a novel by Mervyn Jones, *John and Mary* is the story of twenty-four hours in the lives of a young New York couple who meet, sleep together, and then discover that they're in love. The film begins, in fact, with the sound of John and Mary breathing in bed the morning after they've met and Mary's trying to synchronize her breathing with John's. Yates pays particular attention to contemporary 1969 detail in order to nail down the characters and their New York singles milieu: John's apartment at Riverside Drive and Seventy-seventh; the furniture he designs; the Tom Wolfe and Norman Mailer books on his shelf; her flat on East Thirty-first which she shares with, among others, an underground filmmaker; the pop-art posters; Maxwell's Plum, the bar where they meet; Murray Hill. The characters, unfortunately, are not quite as substantial, a bit bland for two actors so talented at character roles. John and Mary fight, make up, make breakfast, flash back to Ruth, John's ex-girlfriend, and James, a congressman with whom Mary has had an affair that didn't last. But the blandness seems to be Yates' intention in showing how two average people cope with their isolation and even conquer it. (Said Hoffman at the time, "It wasn't the script. I'm not even sure I understand the character. I mean, his life is ordered, he's a good cook, he's aware of clothes, he has a neat apartment. I never lived that way. . . . I wanted to work with Peter Yates.") Farrow wears a brown jumper for most of the film and is alternately pouty, angry, playful, and exhilarated; not for the last time does she make the best of sometimes rather thin material.

John and Mary suffers now from a dated feel primarily because of the flashbacks and editing techniques with which Yates and other British directors (Reisz, Russell, Schlesinger) were experimenting at the time. But the film remains an important time capsule and a modest statement that the true revolutions are not in sex, but in love.

Farrow was poised at this point to do anything she wanted—and she did. Her commitment to family and to a full life, not merely one in front of the cameras, took her to England, where she married André Previn. It was at this juncture, however, that Farrow made her first career misstep. *Rosemary's Baby* had perhaps had the unfortunate effect of typecasting Farrow, unfairly, as a gawky, helpless victim, and after a two-year hiatus, Farrow re-created an unattractive variation on this role in the television film *See No Evil*. Filmed in Berkshire, the movie is a pale imitation of the Audrey Hepburn thriller *Wait Until Dark*, about a blind woman terrorized by a crazed killer. This image would dog her over the next decade, all the way through 1981's *The Haunting of Julia*, a muddy, would-be Gothic psychological horror film about a woman possessed (or not) by the spirit of her dead daughter (as would her being cast in vaguely "English" roles, a problem she would not kick until the Woody Allen films).

Although perhaps an acting exercise for Farrow that enabled her to remain in England close to Previn and her new family, *See No Evil* doesn't compare well even to its descendants, *Friday the 13th* and *Halloween*. The film begins with a series of heavy-handed images meant to tell us that society is violent (a marquee reading "The Convent Murders" and "Rapist Cult," a toy rifle, combat magazines,

the headline "Machine Guns Blaze in Attack," and a stab-
bing on television), and then makes the usual association
with loose morals and loose sex. Much is made of the
poor, blind Mia, who looks more and more like a blue
baby as the film goes on, finding the dead bodies of her
family all over the house, then stepping on glass, stumbling
through a wood and being thrown into a goopy clay bed
("The old clay bed!") by a band of gypsies who are hiding
the psychopathic murderer. Lawnmowers stand out as
metaphors for violence, and it is generally not Mia's day.
She is saved in the end by her veterinarian boyfriend in his
pickup truck.

Why Farrow made this film is a mystery, but it shows
that at this point her highest priority was family. Although
she worked consistently over the next few years under
internationally acclaimed directors like Claude Chabrol
and Carol Reed, her career began a kind of hibernation
here that would last until she reemerged ten years later in
full flower in the Woody Allen films.

Carol Reed's *The Public Eye* (1972) finds Farrow, Reed,
and author Peter Shaffer (*Amadeus*), on whose 1963 one-
act this is based, in a decidedly minor key. Farrow plays
Belinda Sidley, the wife of Charles Sidley (Michael Jayston), an accountant too immersed in his work to have time
for her. Belinda goes for long walks, day and night, and
Charles hires detective Cristoforou (Topol) to tail Belinda
to her presumed affair. But Belinda is just lonely, and
gradually Cristoforou finds himself falling in love with
her. Reed, as in many of his other films, enjoys slyly showing us an "innocent," here the detective, getting all too
knowingly involved in a predicament that he refuses to
admit is a little over his head. Farrow performs pleasantly
in what is essentially a light chamber piece.

Claude Chabrol's *High Heels* (1973) was a departure for Farrow in that she spoke French throughout the film. Although Farrow is excellent, once again she is cast in the kind of gawky, awkward role that would weigh down her career in the 1970s.

High Heels finds a deceased Jean-Paul Belmondo narrating in flashback the tale of his search for an "ugly" woman—a search with a double motivation: a defense against rejection because Belmondo isn't that great-looking himself, and a method of hiding his ambivalence about being attracted to beautiful women with no regard whatever for their character. But Belmondo and his buddies make a game out of it: who can bed the ugliest girl? Belmondo claims to look for "moral beauty."

Farrow, a fellow tourist in Tunis whose car is jammed in the middle of town, is exactly the "ugly" girl he is looking for. Belmondo takes her to bed almost as a dare to himself, and then is shocked to find out this has been her "first time"—a fact that causes him to become even more obsessed with her. But shy, owlish Farrow insults him by leaving him money on the night table. Belmondo finds her and tells her, "You've become ugly for the first time because you've made me not want you," which is, naturally, Belmondo's definition of objectively ugly.

Back in Bordeaux, where Belmondo is in medical school, he runs into her. Farrow turns out to be the daughter of his supervising doctor, who has great respect for the man who took his "ugly" daughter's virginity and courts Belmondo "with all the precision with which he would perform a kidney transplant." Unfortunately, the "gorgeous" Laura Antonelli, Farrow's sister, shows up at their wedding in a tight leotard and leather miniskirt and looks pretty good next to the bespectacled and bucktoothed Farrow. Everything else goes to hell. Belmondo systematically knocks off a series of Antonelli's boyfriends, and Farrow stands idly by at the funerals while Belmondo holds her sister up and tries to comfort her and coax her out of catatonia. Belmondo diagnoses another boyfriend as syphilitic and announces it to friends and neighbors. Belmondo finally has his affair with Antonelli, even though he feels guilty because Farrow got a "B.A. at eighteen, then a degree in science. Then a thesis on primitive Dutch art." Belmondo gets Antonelli pregnant, but Farrow ultimately turns the tables on him with the help of another doctor, with whom it turns out she has been having an affair all along. By the end, at Belmondo's funeral, Farrow is no longer the bookish "ugly" girl but has turned into a sort of voluptuous demon.

High Heels is one of those French films often described as a "delicious romp," and, in fact, the film has its moments. It is a credit to Farrow that she once again stars in a subversively feminist film, like *Rosemary's Baby*, without even the glamour she was allowed in the earlier film. Chabrol shows us a man who becomes a gross, comedic cartoon of himself because he refuses to admit and continues to rationalize his own ambivalence about women, and Farrow is the nerdy, cartoonlike victim of his rationalization, who in the end shows her real strength. Nevertheless, although once again Farrow's ability to make us sympathize with, not merely pity, a character shines, this film in which Farrow looks continually dowdy and lost did not do a great deal for her public image.

The glamour of *The Great Gatsby* (1974)—with its Cartier jewels, Barbara Matera hairstyles, costumes by Theoni

V. Aldredge, and an entire line of fashion by Ralph Lauren—certainly helped to reclaim Farrow's image in the public eye, but it had other drawbacks.

Farrow was the perfect casting choice for the role of Daisy Buchanan; there was simply no one else who could have conveyed F. Scott Fitzgerald's character in all her frothiness, breathlessness, and, ultimately, flakiness. As Nick Carraway, the narrator, says in the novel, "She's got an indiscreet voice. . . . It's full of—" Responds Gatsby, "Her voice is full of money." Farrow resembled, and in the film incarnated, Daisy in every possible way. Indeed, each of the casting choices—Robert Redford as Gatsby; Bruce Dern as Daisy's husband, Tom; Sam Waterston as Nick; Lois Chiles as Jordan Baker, Daisy's confidante and Nick's lover; Karen Black as Myrtle Wilson, Tom's "sweetie"; and even Howard da Silva as Meyer Wolfsheim, Gatsby's "business connection"—was impeccable.

Unfortunately, impeccable casting, impeccable costumes, hairdressing, art direction, photography, locations —even a script by Francis Coppola—do not a masterpiece make. Impeccability may, in fact, have been its downfall, in the absence of any true understanding of the book.

Farrow later commented that Daisy had been extremely difficult to play given how thinly written the part was, and this points to a major flaw in the film's execution. Fitzgerald's characters, with the exceptions of Nick and Gatsby, are indeed "thinly" drawn from a psychological standpoint. In Fitzgerald's vision of America, however, they do fit perfectly, are as whole in and of themselves as they need be; what anchors them is Fitzgerald's conception of the darkness just under the glitter and gloss of the American dream. This conception is entirely missing from the film.

Coppola's script concentrates so excessively on dupli-
cating the actual narrative events of the novel—and in this
it is extremely faithful—that the all-important undertone
is lost. Jack Clayton, a director of character and close-ups,
piles detail upon lush detail but is ill suited to capture
Fitzgerald's elusive spirit. One gets the impression that had
Coppola directed it himself (he, perhaps presciently, turned
it down), the film might have reached for Fitzgerald's vision, but Clayton handled Coppola's already excessively
literal script on a completely literal level.

The major flaw in the script is the elimination of Gatsby's
all-important subtext—with the exception of his love for
Daisy. By letting the story drift from its moorings in Fitzgerald's dark vision of the American dream, Coppola,
Clayton, Evans, et al. essentially turn a profound vision
of America into a story about adultery among the rich, a
story perhaps familiar to Hollywood moguls, but not to
the American public. Coppola replaces the section of the
book about Gatsby's past with scenes between Gatsby and
Daisy, certainly necessary in this context, in which Farrow
must explain the new crux of the film—that she originally
left Gatsby because "rich girls don't marry poor boys."
Although Farrow and Redford and everyone else involved
seem to be doing their best, these scenes, like the rest of
the film, seem lumbering, like some giant last gasp of the
old studio system—which this film, in fact, represented.
Each scene works as a replica of Fitzgerald's rendering of
it, but the whole is much less than the sum of its parts. A
viewer uninitiated in Fitzgerald might well see *The Great
Gatsby* and say, "Huh?" and more's the pity. The Gatsby
team might have learned the lesson found in Polanski's
Rosemary's Baby that details must add up to something.

Farrow is thus perfect—yet her performance suffers accordingly. Like everyone else's performance, it's isolated, not part of a coherent web. Under that diaphanous, fluttery silk hat, Daisy is just Daisy—not part of Fitzgerald's swirling, nonstop America of the '20s. Daisy's lines like the one about her little daughter, "I hope she'll be a fool—that's the best thing a girl can be in this world, a beautiful little fool," which is given an ironic cast in the book, is, like so many other lines in the film, delivered straight, and Farrow is stuck with it.

Nevertheless, Farrow's performance is a triumph despite the handicaps, as are the performances of the other actors. Only Redford, again the perfect choice for the role, is stiff, robbed as he is of any meat in Gatsby's character. Farrow sparkles whether wearing a crazy silver-blue sequined head wig or floating and fluttering on that famous couch in the story's opening sequence. We don't get to see Gatsby's dream, but we do see everything as "dreamy," and that is particularly flattering to Farrow as the pink-and-white dream of a transplanted Kentucky belle. A few shots of Farrow make her look anorexic, particularly in the private scenes with Redford, but this may simply be a sign of Farrow under the strain of a difficult production. As well, as in *See No Evil* and *High Heels*, Farrow's character is desexualized, unfortunately so, because Farrow, as her earlier and later films show, is not unsexy. Here Gatsby and Daisy's love is oddly chaste—all idyllic, sunlit romance and no passion, again more a sign of the juice taken out of the story than of a lack of chemistry between Redford and Farrow, which would have been possible under the right circumstances.

Farrow captures effortlessly the neurasthenia behind Daisy's flightiness and fancifulness, and gives us as definitive a Daisy as we're ever likely to see, just as Waterston

gives us the definitive Nick, da Silva the definitive Wolfsheim, and so on. In fact, the perfection of Farrow's performance, those of others and so many of the details in this
film are all the more painful for taking place in what is
essentially a heavily populated vacuum.

The disaster of *Gatsby*, and perhaps the vast difference
between the hype and the reality—*Time* had put Redford
and Farrow on its cover with the headline "The Great
Gatsby Supersell," which detailed the marketing of Gatsby
clothing, jewelry, and Teflon cookware—sent Farrow
reeling back to her family and the London stage, and the
Royal Shakespeare Company perhaps relegitimized her in
her own eyes through legitimate theater.

When Farrow did reemerge on-screen, she waded back
in slowly, mainly in ensemble films, most of them trivial.
It was in one sense an admission that she had been away
too long; in another it was a tribute to her congeniality as
an actress. In a third sense, perhaps the ensemble films
were a substitute for a family life rich in both natural and
adopted children but no longer rich in marriage.

In Robert Altman's *A Wedding* (1978), a film that definitively summed up the seventies, Farrow played the small
but significant role of the bride's Raphaelite-beautiful but
almost mute sister who turns out to be pregnant with the
groom's baby. The film ends with Farrow in the doorway
of the house, naked, waving good-bye to the last guest.
Farrow also appeared that year in the negligible *Avalanche*,
with Rock Hudson, probably her least important performance next to her cameo in *Supergirl*. In *Death on the Nile*
(1978), Farrow finds herself in an Agatha Christie romp
as Jacqueline de Bellefort, jilted lover of the man married
to the woman who will be the murder victim, and now
under the suspicion, along with Bette Davis, Angela Lans-

bury, George Kennedy, Maggie Smith, Jane Birkin, and Olivia Hussey, of Peter Ustinov's Hercule Poirot and David Niven's Colonel Race on a first-class steamer headed down the Nile. *Death on the Nile* is notable mainly for its opportunity for Davis and Lansbury to ham it up royally in 1930s period costume, for its lovely photography of Egyptian locales, and for its use of three icons of the '60s—Farrow, Birkin, and *Romeo and Juliet*'s Hussey. Farrow rejoined Lois Chiles from *The Great Gatsby*, and the film was directed in leisurely fashion by John Guillermin, director of Farrow's first film, *Guns at Batasi*. Farrow is, in fact, nominally the star here, and she, like everyone else, seems to be having a good time of it (she gets to stand on top of a pyramid and yell at Chiles and Simon MacCorkindale). Unfortunately, the mystery is far too easy to solve.

Hurricane (released 1979) cast Farrow opposite Timothy Bottoms in a remake of the 1936 potboiler starring Jon Hall and Dorothy Lamour. Farrow was likely attracted to the Bora Bora locale because of her father's great love for the South Seas, but the film, aside from showing us a gorgeous and much fuller Mia in various states of South Seas bathing attire, is more footnote than anything else.

By the end of 1981, Farrow's career as a movie actress seemed to have been painted into a corner. Farrow had received good notices in the Bernard Slade play *Romantic Comedy* on Broadway, but *The Haunting of Julia* represented her worst film to date. A muddled mess involving sadistic murders of forty years before, the death of Farrow's daughter by choking (the Heimlich maneuver appeared to be unknown here), and various seances in her creepy old house, *Haunting* wastes Keir Dullea, thanklessly cast as her sadistic ex-husband, Tom Conti as her nice friend, and particularly Farrow herself. Something had to give.

Oddly enough, Woody Allen, whose life Mia Farrow changed as much as he changed hers, had also hit a dead end. Allen has always sought to resolve his inner conflicts in his films, and since he began collaborating with Mia, those conflicts seem to be much closer to resolution. Tracing the Woody Allen films from the beginning exhibits the beneficial effect Mia had on his personal and professional growth.

From the beginning, Allen's films had been about the perils of assimilation, particularly Jewish assimilation into American culture, in different forms. Sometimes the peril of losing oneself was in a girl, sometimes it was in a romantic revolutionary movement, sometimes it was in the Allen character's own romanticized perception of himself and his city. Even in the "earlier, funny films," as the people who claim to be his fans call them in *Stardust Memories*, the Allen character is constantly looking for a cause outside himself in which he can submerge his identity. In *Take the Money and Run*, a pseudodocumentary which foreshadows *Zelig* and tips us off that Woody was setting out to create some sort of autobiography in his work, the ideal is becoming a criminal, being "on the lam." Of course, a life of crime doesn't work out the way he expects. In *Bananas*, the romantic ideal is leaving crazy, neurotic New York and becoming a true revolutionary in Latin America—but Latin America turns out to be far crazier than New York ever was and sends him running back. *Sleeper*'s utopian future turns out to be just a more messed-up version of the present (the McDonald's sign reads "350 million million million hamburgers sold"); *Everything You've Always Wanted to Know About Sex But Were Afraid*

to Ask turns out to be everything you wish you didn't
know: and war and peace in *Love and Death* turns out to
consist of bonking people over the head with bottles and
muttering epigrams about "wheat." In each film, the romantic battle to overthrow the Latin American dictator,
the futuristic dictator's nose, or Napoleon, is fraught with
more stupidity than the character's roots ever could be.

Annie Hall takes the desire to assimilate, to get outside
one's own pitiful self, a step further: here, the romantic
ideal is real romantic love. Annie, the WASP who likes
corned beef on white bread with mayonnaise, has an anti-
Semitic family and aspires to the "California" lifestyle of
cocaine and Beverly Hills parties, is everything that Allen's
alter ego, Alvy Singer, wants to love and become but, in
the end, can't. Alvy is like the shaggy dog who scratches
and paws at the door of the big house, all the while crit-
icizing himself mercilessly, if hilariously, for wanting to
get in; as Alvy says at the end, quoting the man who is
asked why he doesn't do something about his brother who
thinks he's a chicken, "We need the eggs." In *Interiors*,
Allen embodies that romantic desire to assimilate in a completely desiccated, lifeless WASP family, which must have
life literally breathed back into it by the spunky Jewish
outsider Pearl, played by Maureen Stapleton. In *Manhattan*,
this line of thought reaches its poetic pinnacle: Isaac (Allen)
leaves the seventeen-year-old Tracy (Mariel Hemingway),
the best thing that's ever happened to him, for Mary (Diane
Keaton), an ultraneurotic WASP, because he wants to fit
in with his intellectual friends, only to have Mary return
to Isaac's married "best friend," Yale, who wanted Isaac
to take Mary off his hands in the first place. In the end,
Isaac realizes that what are important to him are his roots:

Groucho Marx, Louis Armstrong, Mozart, Flaubert's *Sentimental Education*, Tracy's smile.

You don't have to try to be somebody you're not, Isaac discovers; and to find faith in yourself, as Tracy admonishes him at the end, "You've got to have faith in people."

By *Stardust Memories*, however, released the same year he met Farrow and a year before *The Haunting of Julia*, Allen's identity crisis had turned bitter. The problem now, as Sandy Bates (the Woody persona's most WASP-ish name to date) discovers, is that the public—read: the harsh, critical, yet funny side of Allen's own personality—doesn't want to hear his new discoveries about life and love. It wants the "earlier, funny" stuff, the nebbishy persona who was always trying to please. His "public" has, in a sense, assimilated him, robbed him of his roots in comedy by adoring and adopting them as their own: celebrity turns out to be just as big a trap as romantic love, New York intellectual snobbery, or wacky quixotic revolutionary movements. Once again, Allen has lost his own identity, but this time there seems to be no way out: if he is funny, he feels he is merely pandering; if he continues his merciless self-analysis, however, he risks becoming the pseudo-intellectual creep he sees in his audiences and fears himself to be, as well as the kind of sick man who pursues dangerously neurotic women. *Stardust Memories* is not a pretty sight, and the only avenue seemed to be establishing a filmmaking ensemble, a new family, as it were, from scratch, on his and no one else's terms.

Mia Farrow's and Woody Allen's deepest needs, then— a stable family environment and a stable working environment—dovetailed, and what has followed has been an extraordinarily supportive and nurturing creative and romantic relationship, one in which they do not depend but thrive on each other.

For Farrow, the pressure of working with Allen for the first time in *A Midsummer Night's Sex Comedy* (1982) was mitigated by its being another ensemble film. For Allen, the pressure of making a film after the two-year hiatus that followed the self-flagellation of *Stardust Memories* was eased by the film's light comedic tone, which incorporated for the first time since *Love and Death* elements of Allen's *New Yorker* pieces—bizarre inventions, table-turning, a turn-of-the-century setting. Although *A Midsummer Night's Sex Comedy* is perhaps Allen's most minor work (it is the only recent film not included in the collections of his published screenplays), it is significant because of Farrow's presence and because, for the first time, Allen is not the sole central character in his own film. Consequently, his neuroses are no longer as central either, and the film has a warm, sunny ensemble feel. Allen's and Farrow's creative family was beginning to coalesce.

Allen cast Farrow against her then-type as Ariel, the often shamelessly shallow beauty whom Allen's inventor Andrew has always been infatuated with, now at the expense of his marriage to lovely Mary Steenburgen (in a sense playing a fictional version of Farrow). Andrew finally has his passionate and disappointing moment with Ariel, and realizes, for once, that his ideal girl isn't ideal for him at all. Letting go of the ideal enables him to rekindle his passion for his wife, and everyone, having switched partners, lives (or dies) happily ever after. Farrow and Allen were criticized at the time of *Midsummer*'s release for making Farrow a "pale imitation" of Diane Keaton, and this criticism has some validity. In retrospect, however, it is clear that Allen, rather than merely have Farrow play herself in his life-as-art, has Steenburgen play Farrow and Farrow test her mettle in the role of the woman Allen's character knows he shouldn't like but does, which Diane Keaton played in *Annie Hall* and *Manhattan*, and which Charlotte Rampling and Jessica Harper took on in *Stardust Memories*. In the future, Farrow's roles would be more and more her own.

The sweetness and light of *A Midsummer Night's Sex Comedy* enabled Allen to attack the core of his problem with assimilation, and the result was the Allen film that in fifty years will probably be seen as his masterpiece, *Zelig* (1983). In *Zelig*, Allen creates a character, Leonard Zelig, who doesn't merely wish to assimilate into American or WASP culture or into a relationship, but wants to assimilate completely, in all situations, by turning into everyone he is with—by becoming a human chameleon. Allen confronts the problem of always wanting to be liked, but being too frightened to be liked for one's true self, head-on, finds both the humor and the deeper pain in it, and transmutes his and Zelig's identity crisis into a metaphor for society and the dangers of fascism—the ultimate societal identity crisis. Farrow, appropriately, plays the psychiatrist, Dr. Eudora Fletcher, who nurses Zelig back to a stable and healthy personality and ultimately marries him, a relationship that mirrors, with some exaggeration and considerable humor, Allen and Farrow's own. As Allen has F. Scott Fitzgerald supposedly summing up Zelig, "In the end, it was, after all, not the approbation of many but the love of one woman that changed his life." Allen is at last finding his own stable identity, and Farrow, after years of searching for an elusive balance between the two, has found a family and the beginnings of a more varied acting career.

The catharsis of *Zelig* sets the stage for Allen's four most generous films, *Broadway Danny Rose, The Purple Rose of Cairo, Hannah and Her Sisters,* and *Radio Days,* in which Farrow plays four unique and completely different characters. In *Broadway Danny Rose* (1984), Farrow plays Tina Vitale, the beehive-hairdoed girlfriend, from a family of mobsters, of Lou Canova (Nick Apollo Forte), a fifth-rate Italian lounge singer who wants to become third-rate. Danny Rose (Allen) is his agent with a stable of tenth-rate clients—among others, Barney Dunn, the Puerto Rican ventriloquist; a blind xylophonist; and a lady who plays glasses with water in them. The catch is that Lou is married, and it falls to Danny to escort Tina to the big booking he has arranged for Lou. Danny and Tina end up being chased by Lou's mobster family and fall in love without knowing it along the way. But Lou and Tina, trying to move up in the world—that old Allen desire to be something that you're not—betray Danny by hiring a new agent now that Danny has served their purposes. In the most poignant scene in all of Woody Allen's films, Danny makes Thanksgiving dinner in his apartment for his lonely bunch of tenth-raters and accepts with love and grace his own "tenth-rateness." When Tina comes to apologize he first refuses, then heeds his own Uncle Sidney's advice of "acceptance, forgiveness, and love" and goes to find her.

Farrow's performance is unique, a hilarious and touching dead-on Mafiosa princess, and Allen, significantly, plays for the first time a character who is not a variation of Woody Allen, another good sign. Allen was finally past the identity crisis that culminated in *Zelig,* and Farrow and he were fast creating their own partnership of "acceptance, forgiveness, and love."

The Purple Rose of Cairo (1985), Farrow's real triumph to date and Allen's valentine to her abilities, is a variation on the same theme, if sadder and more autumnal. Here the desire to assimilate, to lose one's identity completely, is the Depression-era waitress Cecilia's wish to step into a motion picture forever. The admission that she can't, and at the same time the acknowledgment that she wishes to, is the source of Allen's wrenching final shot, in which Farrow gazes at Fred Astaire and Ginger Rogers—after actually being able, briefly, to step onto the screen—with a mixture of longing, sadness, memory, and acceptance. *The Purple Rose of Cairo* is, in the end, both a poignant ode to the frailty of human dreams and a cautionary tale about the limited powers of art. Allen and Farrow were beginning to make it look natural to produce a classic every year.

Hannah and Her Sisters (1986) represented a kind of summation for both Allen and Farrow: Allen's acceptance of the frailties and foibles of an extended family in New York and Farrow's portrayal of a character, Hannah, the glue that holds the family together, finally matching to some degree the richness of her off-screen life. *Hannah and Her Sisters* represents the comedic flip side of *Interiors*, in which the three sisters seemed neurotic almost beyond salvation. Here, Allen accepts their and his own limitations, and it ends with Allen's coda that "the heart is a very resilient little muscle." *Hannah* is in fact a sort of stew with elements from several previous Allen films—*Annie Hall, Interiors, Manhattan, A Midsummer Night's Sex Comedy*—but the difference is Farrow's glowing presence at the head of this family and in Allen's life. Allen's character, Mickey, is finally and definitively not the only one who has problems or thinks deeply, and everyone's nuttiness casts a warm, human glow over the proceedings (aided by Carlo di Palma's lush photography, a switch from Gordon Willis's bleaker tones). Allen splits his old persona in two, giving the major part of it to Michael Caine's Elliott, married to Hannah and embarking on an affair with her sister, Lee (Barbara Hershey), while Allen's Mickey has his own parallel search for the meaning of life. (The pundits who say Allen should have consolidated the two characters are wrong.) Through Elliott, Allen perhaps works through his conflicting feelings about Farrow: Elliott's inability to accept her givingness; Hannah's ability to express everyone's needs except her own; Elliott's intimidation by Hannah's resilience; Hannah's condescension to her sisters. There is simply a richness to the entire proceeding, and Allen's screenplay won him his third Oscar. Farrow has never looked more naturally beautiful, and her performance, far from being just "her," is complex, modulated, and detailed.

Radio Days (1987) is the rich fruit of the "acceptance, forgiveness, and love" that was *Hannah and Her Sisters.* *Radio Days* represents Allen's joyous acceptance of his roots and his interweaving of those roots with the outside world through his family's relationship with radio. Farrow, in the parallel "radio personalities" story, plays Sally White, the dumb cigarette girl with the thick Canarsie accent who ends up taking vocal lessons and becoming a Walter Winchell–like radio gossip columnist. Because of the richness and affection that permeate the entire ensemble piece, it is easy to underestimate what is really a virtuoso supporting comedy performance by Farrow, as well as a touching performance by Dianne Wiest as the boy Joey's forever-single aunt.

September (1987) finds Farrow still at the height of her powers as an actress but Allen, for once, faltering. Allen attempts to break new ground in this muted, Bergman-esque chamber piece after having mined his past so thoroughly, but it represents only half a step. Clearly, Allen, having accepted his roots and his family's marginal situation and dependence on the dreams of radio in *Radio Days*, is now working on the real roots of his identity crisis and self-hatred, and the roots can be summed up in one word: Mom. Unfortunately, Allen has for once perhaps geared his exploration of an issue too much toward Farrow, who here plays Lane, the daughter of an actress (Elaine Stritch). Lane's self-destructive behavior is the result of a childhood completely submerged in her mother's unstable and unspokenly cruel identity. One gets the feeling that Allen would be better off leaping into his own troubled relationship with his mother ("the castrating Zionist") rather than diffusing it through Farrow's perspective as the daughter of an actress. Allen bases Farrow's character on Lana Turner's daughter, who stabbed her mother's abusive lover to death, and here the twist is that her mother really stabbed him and made her take the rap for it. But the situation is simply too rarefied and difficult to relate to for the average viewer to feel much of anything. Farrow, nevertheless, is excellent as Lane, a woman in her thirties wracked by the pain her mother has caused her and simply wondering whether the best way to ease the pain and stop the repetition is by ending it all.

Even if *September* is weak, however, once again Allen and Farrow are breaking new ground together. Mia's desires for home and the make-believe of acting have been met in Woody, and Woody has finally found the woman with whom it is safe to make the leap in his odyssey toward acceptance, forgiveness, and love. Woody and Mia have inspired others with their ability to create a family—both on and off the screen—out of their struggles, and it is likely that, now that the birth of their child makes their family complete, they will continue to share with us the joy they share together.

INDEX